Were-Wolf and Vampire in Romania

by
HARRY A. SENN

WITHDRAWN

EAST EUROPEAN MONOGRAPHS, BOULDER
DISTRIBUTED BY COLUMBIA UNIVERSITY PRESS
NEW YORK

1982

*Harry A. Senn is Associate Professor of French and Folklore
at Pitzer College of the Claremont Colleges*

ACKNOWLEDGMENTS

I would like to express my gratitude and appreciation to Alan Dundes for the enthusiasm he created for me in folklore in his quite often spectacular undergraduate and graduate courses in the field; for his advice, support and unfailing interest in my research.

To Cornel Bárbulescu of Bucharest, Romania, I would like to express my immense debt for his guidance through the villages, for invaluable ideas during hours of discussion, and for untiring assistance with tapes, recordings, and confusions.

To IREX, the Fulbright Council for International Exchange, and the Romanian Government, I herewith send my thanks for the funds to carry on research and fieldwork, and to the latter also for special permission to survey the villages.

I am furthermore deeply indebted to the Folklore Centers of Bucharest and Cluj, Romania, for opening their libraries and extensive archive material to me.

Finally, I would like to express my gratitude to Professor Wayland Hand and to the Folklore and Mythology Center at the University of California at Los Angeles for the use of their archives and the study of comparative were-wolf and vampire material.

[iii]

TABLE OF CONTENTS

VILLAGES REPRESENTED IN COLLECTION

INTRODUCTION

The belief in were-wolves and vampires is most closely associated, in the contemporary American mind, with the Transylvanian mountains and forests of Romania. And the larger geographic area of the Balkan peninsula is credited by Ernest Jones (*On the Nightmare*) echoing an early and still much respected study by Wilhelm Hertz, *Der Werwolf*, with providing the fullest development of the beliefs. J.A. MacCulloch in his article "vampire" in the *Encyclopedia of Religion and Ethics* (James Hastings, editor), calls Bram Stoker's *Dracula*, the late-nineteenth-century English novel that has had literally hundreds of adaptations in movies, television and the theater, the "fullest account of all that is believed on the subject in Romania." In as much as our knowledge of vampires comes exclusively from the commercial media, due to the infrequency of the popular superstition in American folklore with the exception of Native Americans, and secondly, since the movies and plays that continue unabated into the nineteen-seventies are almost entirely based on Bram Stoker, an investigation of the pertinence of Stoker's novel with Transylvanian lore is seriously needed.

The living were-wolf that feeds on the dead has historically been closely identified with the revitalized vampire that feeds on the living, especially in cultures where the latter belief is strongly rooted, as for example in Slavic and Greek traditions. In Slavic tradition, in fact, the term that originally designated a were-wolf, *volkolak* ("wolf-haired" or "wolf-skinned") is now mainly restricted to the predominant vampires, and has been adopted for that usage in modern Greece, replacing a term that presently persists only in the outlying islands. The two figures are current in Romania and they are related, but their relationship is to a larger mythological context of nature and the underworld, and they are known by separate terms and distinct behavior.

Although Romania appears to be the "birthplace" of the most famous vampire, we should remember that the were-wolf and vampire constitute two of the oldest figures in world-wide legends and myths. The idea of the dead feeding on the living is found in the Lilats of ancient Babylonia and Assyria, in the Khu of Egypt, and in modern sources such as the Malayan Molong, the Penangelam of Indo-China;

in India, Africa, and South America, in addition to the Finnish Lord
of the Underworld, the Bohemian Mora and the German Alp that all
suck human blood. Conversely, periodic and sacred lycanthropy, in
rare instances coupled with anthropophagy as in Arcadia, was celebrated in ancient Greece and Rome where the wolf was one of the
aspects assumed by the gods of war and death. On the other side of
the Mediterranean, the wolf-god of ancient Egypt acted as a guide
for the souls of the dead in their voyage to the other world. In Northern Europe, the "berserkirs" of Scandinavian mythology and the
Ynglingasaga illustrated another feature of the living shape-shifter
that coincided with prehistorical traditions in India, Iran, Scythia
and Thracia: that of a fierce and frenzied warrior favored by the gods
and destined to take his place in their paradise. In all of the above,
the were-wolves and vampires are fiercesome and terrible creatures.
But most of these were-wolves and vampires come from mythology
and legend. As such they took their place in an overall body of beliefs
and stories, and were thought to exist in the same way that the ancient Romans affirmed that Romulus and Remus were suckled by a
she-wolf, that the Greeks faithfully honored the belief in the minotaur and the Theban sphinx, and the Icelanders suspected that a "retired" berserkir named Kveldulfr was still coursing through the woods
as a wolf in the evening while his visible body dozed. Moreover, in
times and cultures where the mythology of warrior fraternities or
spring fertility festivals combined the wolf, horse, and the dead with
the protection and rejuvenation of the community, lycanthropy and
spirit possession enjoyed a rationalized function in the society.

In the Romanian traditions as in any given encompassing mythological context, there is an entire corpus of beliefs and legends that
explains the existence of were-wolves and vampires, that relates them
to the surrounding natural and human worlds, and that places them
squarely in the above mythological group. Although lacking data and
first-hand knowledge, I suspect that this is true also for the compre-
hensive lore of Greek, Russian and Hungarian village life. In any case,
Romanian were-wolves and vampires, in the context of their folklore,
have as much in common with the "vampires" of the annals of crime,
literature and perverted personalities as Jack The Ripper has with
the Theban Sphinx, or Freud's "Wolf Man" and his father has with
King Minos and the minotaur.

Today, after the prosecutions inspired by the inquisition of village
lore, fertility rites and magic as Devil-worship; after vampire "epidemics" attested to by ecclesiastical courts and judges that lasted
well into the eighteenth century—in 1720 a were-wolf was executed

in Salzburg, Austria, and in 1732 fourteen books were published on the subject of vampirism in Germany alone—the were-wolf and vampire persist as behavioral models in the imagination of individuals with disturbed psyches and stunted sexuality, as fiction anti-heroes of the poets and writers descended from the Marquis de Sade, and as literary case studies of "extraordinary phenomena."

Nineteenth-century romantic and symbolist literature seized upon this metaphor of an irresistible lover of sinister charm and fixed gaze who sucks away energy, ambition or even life, in, for example, Byron's *The Giaour*, Goethe's *Braut von Korinth*, the first literary retelling of the vampire legends of the eighteenth century, Hoffmann's tales of the *Serapion Brethren*, Gauthier's *La Morte amoureuse*, the inspiration for which came from Goethe's earlier story, Merimée's *La Guzla*, and in Poe and Baudelaire. The vampire's ashen voluptuousness was a major element in the ideal of accursed poetry and satanic beauty the post-Sade romantics embraced in their revolt against Christian spirituality. Bram Stoker's *Dracula* portrayed a diabolical monster with mysterious powers who hypnotically seduced virginal maidens and made them his increasingly lifeless but willing slaves; the master was accompanied by previously acquired disciples of beautiful women using their sexual charms for anal-sadistic purposes. But the latest interpretation from Broadway is the promise of everlasting non-death (or "undeath") by a deranged but cool demon to prospective followers who, by the same token, also abandon the experience of life.

Psychological analysis of the vampire fantasy centers on the character of inverted and infantile sexuality. To believe in and relate stories of suave gentlemen, risen from the dead, who seduce their victims in order to suck their blood by means of a mysterious kiss on the neck derives, in Ernest Jones' view, from guilty sexual wishes projected on the dead which originate in infantile incestuous wishes. And the movement from blood-sucking to the devouring lust of the were-wolf corresponds, in the same view, to the development from the first to the second oral stage of infantile sexuality—a stage not surpassed by an individual whose fixation is fused, in later years, to older, more adult sexual capabilities. This reading of the vampire and were-wolf figures has, it seems to me, a reasonable and suitable application to the figures that we are familiar with in films and plays. So too, the appeal of the latest adaptation of the Dracula legend which I take to be a promise of personal aggrandizement, heightened potency and the acquisition of supernatural powers.

But what role do they have in the folk traditions of Romanian Transylvania? Are the vampire and were-wolf legends surrogate scenes of perverted sexuality? What elements in the stories are emphasized: the sadistic, the desire for personal potency, the demonic, the erotic?

The fieldwork that I completed in Romania and the conclusions of which I present to you in the following chapters have provided a strikingly different picture of were-wolf and vampire legends that continue in viable traditons. The folk mythology relates these accidents of nature to failures of humanization and socialization in which children may retain some of the features of the underworld they ought to have abandoned when they were born into humanity. Although in some cases the result of a curse or a punishment for the misdeeds of their progenitors, but also the result of the intrusion of mythological beings, or simply, chance, the remnants of the other side furnish them with special powers, for which they are feared, but also with estimable talents, for which they are revered. And the entire phenomenon is regarded as linked to the family, the society, and to religious ritual; that is, there is a mythological context buttressed by communal beliefs that explains, rationalizes and domesticates the outcast maniacs we are accustomed to in western European and American religious history, films, and drama.

FOREWORD

This book began in June of 1975 in a small Romanian village in Bihor county, near the Hungarian border. Under the tutelage of the Institute of Folklore in Bucharest, my colleague Cornel Bărbulescu and I were actively exploring the area and interviewing the inhabitants to collect as many folk-tales as possible and compare them to related French versions—the subject of my research project. To my genuine surprise, almost two-thirds of the stories, anecdotes and legends dealt with wolf-men or women, ghosts, or the walking dead. I was able, upon our return to Bucharest, to locate and study collectins of Romanian folk mythology, including descriptions of the creation of the world and the numerous fairies and mythical figures who preside over the house, the village, the forest, and the cemetery. Later that month, the opportunity arose to attend the Pentecostal dance ritual called the *căluş*, south of Bucharest, in a small community near a state-run collective farm. The sites of the dances, the costumes, gestures, and dance movements seemed to relate the significance of the ritual to the legends of metamorphosis and vampirism of the village in Bihor country at the extreme opposite northwestern diagonal. I published my findings and sought a second opportunity to return to Romania for more field work.

The following chapters are, for the most part, based on the second period of field research in Romania in 1977 between the months of March and September. In the intervening two years since our first extended residence and study of were-beings in legend and ritual, divided between Petroasa (Bihor), and Frățești (Ilfov), it had become clear that if I desired to draw broader inferences for the whole of Romania concerning were-wolves and vampires, I needed to survey a large number of villages in several sections of the country. I chose hamlets made up of 500 to 1000 inhabitants, engaged in traditional occupations similar to the communities where the study had begun. Guided by Cornel Bărbulescu of the Bucharest Folklore Institute, and with the permission of the Ministry of Culture, nearly fifty villages welcomed us, 110 informants invited us into their homes, willingly and generously providing us with folk legends, beliefs, tales, and music, as well as the traditional food and drink of onions, coarse bread, *slănină* (salt pork), *ciorbă* (soup), fried eggs, and roast pork. We covered three areas of north, south, and northwest Transylvania, and one region of northern Moldavia which encompassed the Neamț, Suceava, Botoșani, and Iași counties. Having returned from northwest Transylvania in 1975 with a majority of narratives of werewolves, witches, ghosts and the walking dead, I set out this time first, to verify whether they were as prominent in other provinces of Romania, and second, to gather as much of the social and mythological context of the legends as possible. In other words, I wanted to discover the origin, causes, and roles ascribed to the magical and nightmarish beings by the communities which maintained and transmitted the legends.

Late in the month of May, while the city and government of Bucharest was still recovering from the terror and the effects of the March 4 earthquake, an independent folklorist, Horia Barbu Oprișan, who had published studies of folk drama at the winter solstice and the călușari dance ritual of Pentecost, invited me to survey the northern Moldavian areas just east of the Carpathian mountains with him. We travelled by automobile to the villages where he had himself collected folk traditions of mumming and dressing up in animal costumes, and later made our way north and east to the Russian border before heading south toward the city of Iași. At first we reestablished contact with his previous informants, and subsequently we called on the resident Orthodox Christian priest, interviewing him for information on the subject of the research project, and thereafter, if possible, speaking to other members of the community reputed for their store of narratives and anecdotes. We were greeted, at times, with wariness and mild suspicion, but most often with generous hospitality. In this area, the stories of were-wolves were virtually nonexistent. There were, on the other hand, extensive and varied traditions regarding the living *strigoi* (witch or wizard), and the dead *strigoi* (vampire), reflecting, possibly, the continuous and long-standing contacts this region has had with the Slavic cultures of Poland and the USSR in which the original term to designate a were-wolf (*vukodlak, vlkodlak*) has become restricted to the vampire.

Upon our return to Bucharest following the conclusion of this primary excursion to the world of rural culture, three more trips were planned for Transylvania with my colleague and guide, Cornel Bărbulescu. This time, however, the whole family, my wife and two small children, aged six and eight years, were allowed to accompany us.

Our schedule in this instance was to locate lodging and board in one village for the entire group, interview the best-known tale-tellers there, and thence travel to surrounding villages.

We looked forward to each of our three trips to Transylvania with great excitement and enthusiasm. Although there is a sharp difference between the capital and the rural villages, in that the latter distinctly lack many of the normal urban comforts, there is, at the same time, a democratic and cooperative outlook that makes one feel accepted and at ease. Moreover, there were no shortages of coffee, beer, cola drinks, or sugar—there is never very much of them outside the large urban areas—and thus the periodic surprises of shortages in the city did not occur. The supply of running water was never shut off, as it maddeningly rather often was in the blocks of new construction where our appartment was located; there was a steady source in the nearby well or running stream near the street. There were, furthermore, no lines of people in the stores; the sales personnel were friendly and helpful; and there was no lack of information or a refusal to explain the absence of a product or an official scheduled to perform a service. The mayors and Communist Party cadres were genuinely concerned about the well-being of their community and the problems of the villagers. They worked alongside their neighbors, particularly in times of adversity, and they seemed to be respected by their co-villagers.

In general, the basic conditions of life in the countryside, the earth, water, herding, weaving and farming have changed little over the centuries. And most significantly, the rural people are deeply attached to, and respect their rich and viable traditions of folk belief and religious custom, their regional costumes, folk tales, legends, and mythological figures. A Romanian sociologist has written of the "spiritual technology" that the mythology and magical thought represent; a technology that seeks to associate the village with the "hidden powers that rule the world." But on an every-day level, the villages experience their traditions as a primary bond that unites them in a community. This is reflected in the uniformity and coherence of the beliefs and narratives, as well as the material lore among different age groups in a given village, and, more surprisingly, from province to province, that together constitute Romania's popular mythology. More specifically, I use this latter term to signify the stories and beliefs that describe the origin, cause, function and significance of super-human beings (including saints, fairies, the dead, and magical animals). This mythology has come into conflict with the Orthodox church at times in Romania's history, particularly the ceremonies involving masks. But the disagreements were most often skirted by compromise or absence of truculence. A more significant cause for the harmony between the Church and the rural folkways arises from the nature of the religious institution itself. In Romania, religion is lived as a set of customs and rites that have incorporated or added to other sets of traditions. There is rarely an emphasis on rigid dogma. The Inquisition, for example, never brought its scourge to Romania, nor did witch hunts, torture, and witch trials precede or accompany wars of religion, as was the case in western Europe, and, to a lesser extent in the colonial United States. In sum, the Orthodox Church has shown itself to be a tolerant and open institution through which pre-Christian beliefs and ritual continue thus to coexist with Christian liturgy.

Once we had completed the formalities and obtained the required papers to allow us to remain in the villages for longer than one day, to bring our leased automobile with us, to film, record and photograph our informants and surroundings, we set out. Our first requirement was to report to the district Communist Party headquarters in the target region. There, the credentials were inspected, coffee was served, polite amenities were exchanged, and we continued on to the specific village. Again, the initial obligation was to introduce ourselves to the mayor and party secretary, accompanied at times with plum brandy and a gift for us of fruit or flowers. It was at this time that we learned of important elders in the community who could provide us with the richest variety of folklore. In the first of the succeeding days, the party secretary often escorted us to the village homes, but soon permitted us to travel alone. As Cornel Bărbulescu tacttfully guided our subject to the project at hand, I was, accordingly, given all the opportunity I desired to put questions to our informants, and to interrupt whenever I needed to ask for amplifications and further explanations. My questions, which quite often coincided with those of my colleague, followed an outline of activities, origin, precautions, and attitudes toward were-wolves (*pricolici, tricolici*), witches and the walking dead (*strigoi*):

—Have you seen or heard of any supernatural beings or unusual events that people talk about?

—Have you heard of or seen any people who can change into a wolf, a dog, or other animal? Where and when?

—Have you heard of or seen witches or vampires? Where and when?

—Why do these beings exist?

—Is it a punishment or a curse? Is it related to the violation of a
rule or law?

—What do people think of them? Are they afraid of them? What
do they do to them?

—What do were-wolves, witches, or vampires do? When? Why?

In three months we stayed approximately a week each in four
different villages: Tilișca (Sibiu), Șanț (Bistrița-Năsăud), Josenii-
Bîrgăului (Bistrița-Năsăud), and Suiug (Bihor). The intervening
periods between field trips were passed in the villages that encircle
the capital of Bucharest.

At times two village homes welcomed us and provided us with, respectively, food and shelter. This was the case in Tilișca in southern
Transylvania, where one house maker prepared our magnificent meals
of banquet proportions (she was in fact the local caterer and enjoyed
a high reputation with her neighbors). She applied her artistry on a
wood stove in an outdoor alcove with low ceiling clearance under-
neath the back porch.

In Șanț, north and easterly from Tilișca, our *doamna* tended her
wood stove in a small structure with no windows or chimney in the
sometimes oppressive, hot days of July. Near the "Borgo Pass"
through which Jonathan Harker, Bram Stoker's hero of *Dracula*,
travelled on his way to the infamous vampire's castle, we were received in a very comfortable village house in Josenii-Bîrgăului (the
Romanian version of "Borgo" is "Bîrgău"). The sojourn here was
memorable for the hot indoor bath we enjoyed, especially after my
ten-mile hike to the shepherd's hut on the top of the mountain, and
the two separate rooms with ample beds that were made available to
us. Several villagers took turns creating the dinners for us, and the
three-day stop in that community was disappointingly too short.

In Suiug, in the extreme northwestern county adjacent to the
Hungarian border, I discovered an allergy to goose-down that erupt-
ed during the night of our arrival there. The village household was
again remarkably hospitable and comfortable with a pump to bring
the water into the house and heated baths or showers. There was a
long discussion here with a young teacher from the village who was
invited to share our noon meal, and wonderful repasts with wine or
țuica brandy. Our visit ended here as everywhere with an exchange
of gifts, but in Suiug we were presented a hand-made, long, narrow
rug of the kind used by Romanians to cover the floors of their homes.

Our visit to Șanț was the most extraordinary for us. It included
an accident in which our daughter, aged eight, fell down the well

in the front yard while trying to hang a bucket full of water on the nail at the top. She had cranked up a full pail to wash her doll's clothes. We had left earlier in the morning to buy food, and, in our absence, the hostess of our house and a neighbor rescued our daughter by making her understand to sit on the bucket at the bottom of the twenty-foot pit, and brought her back to the top bruised and terrified, but not seriously injured. During the same visit, we were invited to a picnic-barbecue at the mayor's summer shepherd's cabin. We drove about ten miles past the limit of the town into the mountain valley where he sheltered his herd, and there a sheep was slaughtered, skinned and roasted over a wood fire. The effect of witnessing the entire drama of choosing, killing, and dressing the sheep's meat was indelible to inexperienced city-dwellers like ourselves, and caused us to seek some comfort in the liberally supplied vodka; with later pronounced discomforts. We marvelled at the way in which all the edible and inedible parts of the animal were consumed or utilized to the fullest extent.

A few days before our outdoor barbecue, we had driven to the top of the nearby mountain to a summer vacation camp for a group of adolescents from the Black Sea coast. The children who live normally in the mountains travelled, by the same token we were told, to camps near the Sea. Our hike on the grassy top of the peak and the generous afternoon meal was topped off at dusk by the campers' songs and games, and the ceremony to lower the flag. Before the presentation, however, I was drawn into a rather strained debate in Romanian, with, for all practical purposes, no respite in French or English. A middle-aged woman, a doctor from the capital of the county, who was accompanying the official from the Ministry of the Interior on one of his periodic visits to the region's youth camp, took issue with the propriety of our attire and the quality of American society in general. We were wearing jeans, for the hike and the picnic, and she wore a dress of a rather nondescript model prevalent in eastern Europe. She criticized the self-centered and materialistic nature of Americans generally, the violence of American films (the Buford Pusser story "Walking Tall" and its sequel had been playing to large crowds across the country). The irony of part of our conversation was, incidentally, the intense popularity of blue jeans all over East Europe, and, although our protagonist interpreted our attire as a "sign of the hippy rebellion against American society," jeans probably represent a similar sort of revolt in East Europe. After our comparatively contentious conversation and in the subsequent games and songs, , the previous relaxed socializing with our sponsors and hiking companions dwindled to brief exchanges designed to allow all to keep their distance and yet preserve the fabric of sociability. Such is the influence of Bucharest party officials and their effect on the other members of the society.

CHAPTER ONE

ROMANIAN LEGENDS

The mythical were-wolf figure in Romania, as in other societies, probably resulted from the interaction of human society with wolves and from their traditionally extraordinary behavior. Although this particular predator has long since disappeared from Romania, its legendary ferocity is still recounted in the villages. One source of our fieldwork collection told us how he had seen a single wolf leap over a high wall, usually sufficient to protect the village herds, and, in the space of a few minutes, slaughter seventy-five of the penned sheep. In another instance, the number was eighty-seven. Some of the sheep were saved by the informant's chance arrival, but the surviving remainder of the herd "could not eat for three days." (Tilişca, Sibiu) It is generally related that the wolf will slaughter as many sheep as possible, but will eat only one. There are stories of lone courageous sheep dogs, however, that stand off seven wolves, until other help can arrive, or until they themselves are killed. (Răşinari, Sibiu) The wolves are, for their part, protected by Saints Peter and Andrew; they were perhaps even Saint Peter's creation and are his agents to punish those who, by eating meat, fail to observe properly his feast day. In one tale, the remaining bacon and pork that two young girls had enjoyed on Saint Peter's day, disappeared soundlessly and mysteriously at night during a storm—it was the punishment carried out by wolves for their transgression. (Tilişca, Sibiu) At the risk of his life, a villager was known to enter the forest on the eve of Saint Andrew's feast day to call the wolves to him by howling through a clay pot and distribute smoked meat to them. He sought to propitiate them and mollify their behavior toward humanity. (Bucharest, Ilfov)

The inherent frenzy of the wolf supplies an unnerving edge to the tale of the were-wolf (Thompson motif D 113.1.1) husband who attacks his wife, tears her clothes, but departs without inflicting bodily injury on her. At times she dies from the shock of discovering (by the threads of her clothing in his teeth, H 64.1) the secret identity of her husband. (Related in all areas of Transylvania; see also Reidar

[1]

Christiansen's *The Migratory Legend*, p. 58.) They may, however, remain together, or divorce, or the young woman may return to the refuge of her parents' home.

Nonetheless, a were-wolf may evoke a compassionate response from a worker or camper in the forest. In one popular legend, a wolf emerges from the woods and paces on the far side of a camp fire where food is cooking. The camper shares his *slănina* (pork fat) or bread with the hungry animal that finishes the food and departs. Later in a nearby village, the worker's wares are wholly purchased and he is richly rewarded by a wealthy landowner who confides that he, a were-wolf, had visited the man's camp as a wolf. (Holod, Bihor; Pria, Sălaj)

This particular humanitarian gesture is confined, to my knowledge, to Romania. In other widespread areas of Europe and America, it is considered an act of charity to inflict a wound on the suspected were-wolf, for, by drawing blood from between the eyes, or elsewhere on the head, the enchantment is sometimes broken. In all cases, and Romania possesses its own variants, to draw blood forces the extraordinary animal to regain its human form. (D 712.6)

In northwestern Transylvania, a man or a woman "spinning" in the forest convokes his or her wolf pack, and although a passing villager escapes harm and even death by greeting the wolf leader and referring to the assemblage as "rams" or "sheep," he vows never to return by that route again. (Pria, Sălaj) Another female wolf leader dressed in white presides over a "wolf wedding" as witnessed by a spectator from his tree perch she had menacingly directed him to take. (Pestid, Bihor) The leaders and wolves are said, at times, to hurt only those with whom they have quarreled. (Hidișelul-de-Sus, Bihor)

A were-pig, called a *tricolici* in Șanț, Bistrița-Năsăud, is known to attack indiscriminately on the eve of Christmas or Easter, biting and blocking the way to villagers, and assaulting them as they pass. A passerby on foot, or a nightwatchman most often grabs what is nearest at hand and tries to beat off the animal. Quite often a pitchfork is used and the pig is wounded on the face; the same injury will appear on a man who lives in the town, or on the wife of the village church cantor. An explanation sometimes follows that attributes the "curse" or condition to a little tail at the base of the spine, or to the fact that as a child the adult were-being had been allowed to return to breast feeding after an initial weaning. (Ștupca, Neamț; Șanț and Leșu, Bistrița-Năsăud)

Our informants asserted that when one sees a sinsister-looking dog, one automatically reaches for a pitchfork or a sharp instrument with which to stab it and bring blood forth. The human being within is, in this way, revealed. A strange dog near the cattle or sheep is cause for the villagers to pursue it with their pitchforks. A dog in one legend (Gîrbou, Sălaj) "began to cry like a man as it ran off," wounded; a wolf, who was seen sucking milk from the cows was stabbed, but before dying, it turned a somersault and changed back into a man. (Suiug, Bihor) The transformation does not inevitably take an animal shape; a witch, for example, may become a wheel that errantly rolls through the village. In one such instance, the wheel was captured and an axle was stuck through the hub. Two days later, they found a man "with the axle through his mouth and sticking out his anus." The man asked to be let free and promised never to come back. (Gîrbou, Sălaj)

The unnatural animal is associated with the Devil in one legend of a wealthy property owner of advanced middle age who, after the death of his first wife by cancer, had remarried a young woman "to have children by her" (the emphasis is on his attempt to prolong unnaturally the activities normally associated with a younger age). One night, travellers saw the "Devil" sitting on the gate of the house. They stopped and asked for some food. The young wife climbed up into the attic storage area for supplies and found a large black dog there. Her efforts to wound it with a pitchfork failed, and she also failed to dislodge it. Some time later the wife gave birth to a son, accompanied by a visit of the *ursitoare* or goddesses of destiny. Three days later all the windows and doors of the house blew open and slammed shut. After nine months, the infant boy became covered with fur, stunk like an animal, and died. "The Devil was in that house." (Tilişca, Sibiu)

Several villagers tell how their father or an acquaintance encountered a being that changed its shape before their eyes; a ram, then a doll— on the eve of the Easter holiday (Şanţ, Bistriţa-Năsăud); a pig, then a wildcat, then a dog (Şanţ); a pig that follows the main character of the narrative home, stands on its hind legs and peers through the cracks of the house (Şanţ); or of two horses that suddenly become a man with horses' feet (Holod, Bihor). In Pria, Sălaj, the informant's great-grandfather was threatened by a wolf that had exited from the woods; suddenly a voice called out the were-wolf's name, "Ion Indrioana." The wolf howled, but returned to the forest. In Pestid, Bihor, a man with a large birth stain on the back of his neck was believed to kill the sheep of the villagers who refused to provide him with food.

He protected the son of one specific woman—the narrator, who generally propared more food than she needed and made it available to anyone that asked. The following day after each time she unexpectedly met the man outside the village, she learned that more sheep had been slaughtered.

The unexplained absence of a neighbor from the community may lead others to believe that he is a were-wolf. A mysterious departure for three days of one particular villager drew the account that he ran with wolves and participated in their predatory behavior. Another villager was gone for "two or three years." (Poclusa, Bihor) Or a gypsy is identified as a were-wolf in a specific legend. He had been hired to drive a woman's cart to a market in a nearby village. On the way, he departed suddenly, and, after a ruckus of loud snarling and growling, he returned bloody and disheveled. She was told in the market that her driver was a wolf-man. The narrator of the story added that werewolves are a part of the world—like musicians or dancers; that is, they all possess special talents. (Tilișca, Sibiu) Although gypsies are quite often musicians in Romania, this is the only tale I collected that identified the changeling as a gypsy.

However, a set of special talents may be used for pernicious ends, as in the example of the stranger to Sibiel (Sibiu) who could whistle out snakes from the forest, and carried them around in a pot. He rolled through the village at certain times turning somersaults. At other times he probably roamed as a big black dog. One day he put a mouse into a woman's pot of milk to make her give it to him. He was a robber and a swindler. Another stranger to a community in the county of Bihor, a woman, had a tail, and, after entering the woods and undressing, she used its power to become a wolf. The teller added that there was no scandal or persecution. But also, the village did not want to antagonize and suffer the savage reactions of a wild animal. (Forosig)

An evil man in life will be attended by none save infernal animals after death. A young man was returning from military service. He carried the rifle that he had been issued by the army as he entered a village at sunset one day to find lodging for the night. A village house with a light attracted his attention, and he went in. On a table lay a dead man, but the house was empty. The young soldier climbed into the loft and kept his rifle nearby. At 11:00, the door flew open, and a big dog rushed in. The dead man rose up and the two of them battled furiously until 12:00 when the dog departed. The next day, the young fellow went to the town hall and inquired why they did not watch over and protect their dead. He was told that normally this was indeed the custom, but the deceased was so evil that no one wanted to stand guard over him; "it was the Devil's job." (Şanţ, Bistriţa-Năsăud)

An elderly woman in Pestid (Bihor) summed up the characteristics of the wizard (*strigoi*) which mainly related to milk, blood, and water. Sometimes the witches suck the milk from cows or sheep in the form of a dog or a wolf. (D 655.2; E 251.3.2) Predestined to the condition at birth, due to the presence of the caul, the curse is prevented if the mid wife removes the scum and destroys it. Such a witch may also suck the blood from children until they die. Nevertheless, a wizard-for-work (*strigoi pe lucru*) is regarded as merely a prodigious worker.

Strictly speaking, the mythological being that molests cattle and sheep by stealing their milk, but does not kill or eat them, is categorized as a witch or wizard. They stand apart from were-beings by their preoccupation with milk, the life force of fields, with floods and droughts. In their case, people ascribe to them a larger element of conscious malevolence, but, nonetheless, they may have inherited the predilection for witchcraft behavior, or it may have been their "destiny," as it was for the were-wolf.

The means of obtaining the milk are illustrated in the following stories. In a group of loggers hiking up the mountain to the forest, one of the companions brings milk from a herd of sheep grazing nearby simply by sticking his knife into a tree. Immediately drops of milk, then blood, begin to fall—the latter because the sheep had already been milked. (Tilişca, Sibiu) Another witch could make the milk drip from his attic merely by pointing a knife upward. (Tilişca) In a further instance, a male *strigoi* passed through the village chanting "de aici o ţiră, de aici o ţiră" (from here a little, from there a little), preparing to get the milk from each door. As he walked by a certain household, the owner was relieving himself in the outdoor toilet. The witch's words evoked an impulsive "şi din curul meu" (my ass you will) from him. The passerby remarked "fine," and went on his way. The inhabitant of the house began to bleed from the anus and did not stop. After six weeks he remembered how the blood flow had begun and sought out the witch to make him staunch it. The witch cured him but only with the promise that no more would be said of the incident, and the villager would never again be caught pronouncing that particular imprecation in a similar situation. (Tilişca)

One informant's grandmother had met a *strigoiaica*, a female witch, on the road. The *strigoiaica* told her that if she revealed her secret identity, the grandmother would lose her head. This so terrified her that she would no longer walk home from the train station alone at night. When that witch died, people said that they saw her emerging from the river. (Tilişca) I will return to the river motif shortly, after finishing the group of encounters with the witch.

A witch will often be seen with a horse, moving about in the cemetery. An informant's father had lain down in a graveyard to rest one night when he perceived a woman riding a horse. He followed her until she stopped and admonished him to keep silent about this meeting, in return for which she promised him that his property would always be safe from storms and lightning. This same mysterious personage could also bring milk from the rafters of her house by sticking a pitchfork into the ceiling (Tilişca) Another informant's father discovered two horses turning around a cross on a grave. The horses spied him and pursued him. He fell, and they were upon him, rearing up and trampling down. He got up and fled again, making the sign of the cross with his tongue. The horses turned away, so he wheeled around after them, picking up a stick. As he brandished his stick, charging after, the animals started to turn somersaults and changed into two big millstones that rolled resoundingly down into the valley and disappeared. (Şanţ, Bistriţa-Năsăud)

On the eve of Saint George's feast day, a cart wheel appeared in the village of Corneiu (Cluj) and whirled down the street. Some young boys captured it and tied it up on the wall of a house. Two days later, they discovered a woman from a neighboring village hanging on the wall in place of the wheel. They recognized her and realized that she was a witch.

Romanians assert that witches bathe in the river in the dead of winter even with a layer of ice on the water, late at night, or very early in the morning. If discovered, the witnesses are warned never to repeat what they have seen. (Gura Rîului, Sibiu)

A cow may be so ensorceled that it will walk to a witch's house to be milked. (Josenii-Bîrgăului, Bistriţa-Năsăud) But when a cow ceases to give milk, the villages have a few charms of their own to break the spell. An informant's father-in-law used a few branches from a hazel tree to slap the back of the cow, as he chanted "I beat the witch; I beat the witch." Next, they unfurled a string and made the cow walk over it. The teats came unblocked. (Sibiel, Sibiu) A woman from Tilişca had consulted another witch in a Saxon German village for magic to bring her cow's milk back. She took some garlic, pork grease with mold on it to a white witch (*vrăjitoară*) who intoned a spell. At that very moment, the cow began to eat. Not long afterward, something frightened her horse, and it broke out of the barn. The next morning, the cow began to give milk. It should be noted here that generally horses are considered vulnerable to the effects of powers or spirits; the villagers will, for this reason, hang a red tassel around their horse's left ear for protective purposes.

One can be a witch and still function as an important member of the community. One boy was born with a tail, in eastern Romania, and was considered a witch by his community. Nevertheless, he grew up to become a respected property owner in the village. (Hangu, Neamţ) And yet, if a witch's offense is sufficiently grievous, as was the villain's act who ripped out the heart from a black lamb, burned it to cinders, and mixed the ashes into the food of the other sheep, it may be more severely punished. The sheep went mad; they stopped giving milk and fled from one another. And when the shepherds found the guilty party, they killed him. (Tilişca, Sibiu) A grave that had been disturbed revealed a body whose fingers and toes had been cut off. The following Sunday in church, the priest announced that whoever was responsible for desecrating the grave and despoiling the body would die all alone, surrounded by crows. At that moment, a woman fell down dead, and crows flew into the church and hovered over her. (Şanţ, Bistriţa-Năsăud)

The legends relate several causes for the dead to return from the grave to haunt and bedevil the living. In one family, the seventh of nine sons died by drowning. He could be heard after dark and until midnight in the house making noises. Our informant's grandfather said that his family felt his brother's presence in the house, nothing more. (Sălcea, Broşteni) A man who had been killed by stabbing, came back each night from the cemetery to look for his wife. He traveled in his coffin like an automobile. The neighbors simply told him that his family had moved away, and he stopped coming back. (Şanţ, Bistriţa-Năsăud) It may be necessary, to gain relief from the reversions of a vampire to disinter the body and plunge a nail through the heart (E 442); as in one case when "the heart was not dead." (Tilişca, Sibiu) In even those instances when the vampire does not threaten overtly anyone in the village—as, for example, a wizard-for-working—the suspected vampire will be dug up and a stake pounded into his heart. (Marginea, Bihor)

The entire community may assist a neighbor who is threatened by
the dangers of the undead. A notary's servant who discovered a dog
sucking milk from cows, killed it with a pitchfork. The priest of the
town gave him explicit directions, first, to buy new clothes, paying
the first price asked, second to bury the witch without a casket, and
last, to watch over the body for three nights. The first night, the
vampire came out of the grave, but the young man hid behind the
church cross, and she did not find him. The second night, two witches
came out, but he hid behind the church altar. The third night, three
witches emerged and looked until they discovered him, but not until
it was 3:00, and they had to return to their graves. The appointed
time had elapsed, and the servant fled to his house where he is now
married and has children. (Holod, Bihor)

The last tale of a vampire relates the story of a young woman who
died from the shock of her father's death. Nevertheless, she reverted
to life and visited her former suitor in the shape of a wolf. In fear of
his own life, the young man beat her with a stick, for which she reproached him later, for he had left her henceforth unable "to be a
true woman"—that is, to conceive children. (Pria, Sălaj)

The last category of legends in my collection recounts the deeds
of magic dragons about three feet long that fall to earth from the
midst of a whirlwind, or that reside in high mountain lakes. A huge
dragon is said to have entwined itself around an entire village church
in the town of Greabla, locking its jaws on its tail. The parishioners
escaped through the windows and moved their homes to a new town
of Brebești. (Tilișca, Sibiu) One informant's father witnessed an incident in which a man dressed in black, reading from a large book,
called a dragon out of Lake Cindrelu, mounted it and flew off with
it. As they departed, rain and hail poured down. (D 199.2.1; tale-
type 326C)

Another powerful serpent, five meters in length, had been found
during the festival of Shepherds on Saint Elijah's feast day. The sheep
dog that killed the dragon lost its own life in the battle as the serpent
coiled itself around the dog's body. The shepherd owner of the dog
died a year later himself on the anniversary of the encounter. (Tilișca,
Sibiu)

One woman from Sibiel told of how her father had heard the voices
of the *iele*—fairies—one night as he was sleeping on the porch that
runs along the front of the village houses. The fairies invited him, in
song, to come to them and make them some bricks for building. He

refused, saying, that he had to care for his own animals. He never slept on the porch again. (Sibiel, Sibiu)

The legends, in summary, illustrate the belief that dragons, witches, were-wolves, and vampires exist and interact with the inhabitants of Romanian villages at certain times and in certain ways. The villagers' reaction to them is to acknowledge that the world is made up of very different beings and to accept the reality of their existence without actively seeking to rid the community of their presence. That is to say on the one hand, that the rural people avoid aggressive confrontation with threatening figures, because they accept an established state of reality, and they know that there is an inevitability in their occurrence. In this way, the unorthodox but living members of the human community continue to reside and to pursue their life's occupations even though they may clash with the well-being of their neighbors. In other words, the abnormal, like their co-villagers, are a part of a larger unity beyond the power of the community itself. Thus confrontations are avoided, but, on the other hand, combat is accepted in self-defense and all strength and abilities are utilized for one's protection. The village folk traditions counsel precaution and awareness of the forces and beings that inhabit the world at the same time that they explain the causes for the order of things, and, in extreme situations, describe the methods one must use to preserve and protect one's self, the family, and the village. Finally, one accepts the inevitable and pursues one's life, drawing on the very same extra-human unity, that lies at the basis of the community's view of the world, for meaning, strength, and dignity in the face of immediate adversity that is, however, they believe, of limited duration.

CHAPTER TWO

SOCIAL STABILITY WITH WERE-WOLVES AND *STRIGOI*:
THE ROMANIAN MODEL

After completing two six-month periods of study and fieldwork in Romania in 1975 and 1977, the approximate one hundred and fifty legends of were-wolves, *strigoi*[1] and wolves, and the several hundred expressions of folk beliefs that I returned with have convinced me that the Romanian village culture possesses a sensible and balanced method of presenting and explaining the existence of beings that are the object of horror, commercial titillation, and psychiatric therapy in other societies.[2] Were-wolves, vampires, and witches have been linked historically in less-developed and developed societies alike, and, although their behavior is markedly separate in Romania, they share one common term, and the same set of circumstances are thought to create them. Their existence is ascribed to abnormalities of birth and death; explained by the failure to observe specific religious taboo or to successfully socialize the infant, by the intervention of mythological figures, the chance overlapping of the natural and human realms, or the failure to achieve the complete integration of the deceased into the realm of the dead. In effect, the were-wolf, witch, and future vampire are not totally "humanized" beings, but bear the mark of the other world, that is, a little tail (*codiţa*), or are born with the caul. They can utilize the power of wild animals because they are supernatural beings intermediate between human society, nature and the magical chthonic realm of fairies and the dead. Insofar as the were-wolf and witch are members of the village, and although they may constitute a danger to others and to their neighbors' domestic animals, they are not the object of "witchhunts" or scapegoating. In the legends and memorats, those believed to be witches are treated with caution and even deference by their fellow villagers. Fundamentally, the living (*vii*) *strigoi* is at times, but not exclusively, in cases of quarrels and resentment, an aggressive danger to the villagers' cattle, which they may steal, eat, or rob of milk, or to cultivated fields, from which they may sap the reproductive force.

They are believed capable of causing floods or droughts, and of destroying a woman's breast milk. For these reasons, the term "witch" best describes them. The *strigoi mort* or deceased witch, but by extension any reanimated dead, that returns from death to wreak harm on the living, is known to us as a "vampire." The latter, notwithstanding western novels, films and plays, may also be motivated by the desire to care for surviving family members or to pursue the pleasures and toils of life to which they were singularly suited and from which they were unwillingly wrenched. The *pricolici* or "inverted wolf" is another periodic danger to the community, but when not prey to the metamorphosis, one who is also considered to have his place and to perform other necessary functions for the village. The legends unanimously recount encounters with humans who have taken a wolf form, or who claim to have that power. There are none told by self-proclaimed were-wolves. Human wolves, in Romanian tradition, are most often the victim of a prophecy or a punishment for the transgression of a religious taboo by their parents. Thus, the reaction of their fellow villagers is sometimes sympathy and respect, as well as fear and apprehension. Nevertheless, the legends teach us that if attacked, one has the basic right to fight back with all necessary force. But to kill a were-wolf, for example, for no overt cause brings punishment to the slayer, and to help a wolfman to break his enchantment can bring rich rewards. In the case of witchcraft, one can call on another wizard for countermagic, or use the preventive powers of plants and ritual. For the deceased witch or "vampire" who has abandoned the human state and is universally shunned, the solution, in addition to pre-burial protection, relies on plunging a stake or nail through the body.

The difference between the attitudes toward the origin and cause of were-wolf and *strigoi* creatures as they endure in Romania and the Inquisition and witch trials of Europe and the United States, for example, lies therefore in the body of beliefs and practices of Romanian society that I define as "cultural context"; that rationalize and domesticate these fearsome beings, and the contrary custom of assigning their cause to the misguided souls of individual members of the society. The Romanian folk example stands nearer the tribal models found for example in Africa where such scholars as Edward Evans-Pritchard, Philip Mayer, and Max Marwick discovered that witchcraft beliefs and accusations fulfilled an important role in the stabilization of the society.[3] Evans-Pritchard opened the general study of the role of the irrational in society in *Witchcraft, Oracles and Magic among the Azande* and found that sorcery was a function of "situations of misfortune." He pointed out, however, the positive effect of settling grudges in the open and providing a formula for action in the midst of misfortune. Philip Mayer in his inaugural lecture, "Witches" at Rhodes University, argued that witchcraft beliefs in African communities before the invasion of missionaries and western technology represented a domesticated species, unlike the wild and savage European type. Max Marwich, *Sorcery in its Social Setting: A Study of the Northern Rhodesian Cewa*, emphasized the normative and explantory functions of witchcraft. It is difficult to say to what degree the inner predispositions of the developing personality or the forces and requirements of the surrounding society hold the primary role in the formation of the individual. Nevertheless, for the social group to persist in a relatively peaceful state, the socialization process, or specific institutions must exist to provide the possibilities for integration of resentments, grudges, and anti-social aggression. Certain societies emphasize the influence of socialization over individual life history and consequently view the significance and cause of were-wolves and witches in exceedingly different manners. Why Romanian folk beliefs should demonstrate such a great similarity to a few non-western cultures and an accordingly wide dissimilarity to the devil-crazed practitioners of western Europe and to films of diabolical men and beautiful sadistic women is what we will examine in this paper.

A 1936 study of were-wolves that, by negative comparison, may offer a key to understanding the Romanian example is found among the Navaho Indians of North America. In it, William Morgan asserted that the cultures that transmit in their belief systems and narratives supernatural figures such as were-wolves and maintain preventive or curative rituals in accordance with such beliefs, will give a "sensible validity to such imagery and fears when they involuntarily appear in an individual."[4] Other societies, on the other hand, that have eliminated such figures from their traditions and institutions risk an unending series of social disruptions and violence. Morgan argues that the belief in human wolves originates primarily in the personality of the individual member of the Navaho tribe—and thus within the individual personality—for the imagery present in some of the stories he collected of were-wolves or that related specific were-wolf behavior, such as despoiling corpses or murder and cannibalism are not, in his opinion, "characteristic" of Navaho culture as a whole. (p. 11) Without entering into a discussion of direct or indirect reflections of ethnological phenomena, this may represent his own intellectual biases,

or it may be a true image of Navaho society. In either case, the absence
of validation of such fears in the society would place the sole responsibility for treating the roots of the phobias on the person who is
afflicted with them (without the aid of psychological institutions).
Such a hypothetical situation may, in reality, explain the severity of
Navaho human wolf fears and witch accusations which attained a
level of near hysteria in later years. In general, Morgan sees wolf-man
stories arising from the distortions that are produced by the continued
repression of individual sadistic impulses; after a certain point the
continually recurring fantasy image becomes semi-human and semi-
animal. (p. 6) For the basis of the sadistic impulses themselves, he re-
fers us to Ernest Jones (*Nightmare, Witches and Devils*, later titled
On The Nightmare); they are rooted in the œdipus complex; that is in
the sadistic eroticism and jealous hostility aroused against the respec-
tive parents.[5] From this point of view, then, such products of fantasy
and imagination not related to specific institutions or ritual originate
in individual psychology. And since they are therefore not integrated
into the general view of the world, nature, and community, it seems
likely that the projections could hardly diminish.

The belief in human wolves among the Navaho, after Morgan's
fieldwork, retained a particular form and was actively perpetuated;
for other "Navaho wolf" stories were collected and published ten
years later by Clyde Kluckhohn and Dorothea Leighton (*The Navaho*).
In this latter study, in contrast to William Morgan, the existence of
the human wolf is believed to be centered within the social system
and the theory of the supernatural of the tribal culture itself. Through
witchcraft, evil men, active mainly at night, are believed to be able
to produce illness and death and obtain the property of those whom
they hate. They often wear the hide of a coyote or wolf and are called "human wolves," or "Navaho wolves."[6] Witchcraft belief is extra-
ordinarily persistent, and, in the absence of specific Navaho explanations beyond an "evil nature" or hatred, Kluckhohn and Leighton
attribute the role of these stories to the release of tensions between
brother and sister, that is of jealousy and incest attraction, and, in a
wider context, to a safety valve for the high level of anxiety, worry
and uneasiness present in the society at large. The rampant insecurity
is probably due to the "bewildering change" the entire culture was
undergoing and which brought inevitable personal and social disap-
pointments and an accompanying tendency to scapegoat. (p. 234, 233)
Furthermore, although taboos and ritual regulations have brought
some security and the possibility of avoiding harm, they "pile up

additional apprehensions and hazards," like a neurotic's reliance on an obsessive set of procedures. (p. 234) More ominously even, "talk about witches commonly has a violent quality completely out of proportion to the involvement of the speaker in that particular case. The killing of witches is characteristically messy and brutal, even on the part of those who are not avenging some near relative or close friend. Witches, in other words, are scapegoats." (p. 246)

The witchcraft accusations and beliefs, in the authors' eyes, help Navaho society as a whole continue as a "going concern," but hardly seem, in this instance, an efficient or satisfying method for this purpose. Such beliefs probably create as much anxiety as they relieve, and, in attributing individual insecurities and hostility to an outcast witch beyond the pale, produce a great deal of directed aggression. They arose, in Evans-Pritchard's terminology, from situations of misfortune, but, far from finding resolution in the open, they have increased along with the level of anxiety and aggression. There has been no formula for communal action in the midst of misfortune.

It seems that there are more successful social models in Sub-Saharan and East Africa that are closer to the prevailing beliefs in Romanian villages. In witchcraft-dominated cultures, as Mary Douglas observes, all evil is assigned to abnormal neighbors, and Sartre's dictum that "hell is other people" prevails.[7] But this axiom is not universal, rather, according to Claude Levi-Strauss,[8] it is a specific ethnographic comment on a particular culture. In East Africa, for example, Dinka concepts of witchcraft reflect a normal assessment of human nature and a continuing self-appraisal, the outcome of which is that the Dinka are strongly reluctant to call any man a witch; "for any man who easily thinks himself hated is one who easily hates, and... a man who sees other as bearing malice toward himself is one who himself feels malice.[9]   The concepts of witch accuser and victim lead the Dinka to look within themselves before bearing an accusation against someone else.

On the opposite coast, in western Cameroun, the Banyang likewise consider the possible implications of the accuser in an inquiry about evil actions. All members of the tribe are considered potential malefactors of witchcraft to the extent that all people possess "were-animals" (babu). The function of the were-animals range from making manifest the powers and abilities conceived in a most anti-social passion, to representing, as a sort of metaphorical description, a person's individual talents. Malcolm Ruel, whose research these comments reflect, explains: "Strength in fighting or carrying loads, the ability to slip out of an opponent's grip, to jolt an opponent into releasing his hold, or fly up out of a dangerous situation, to burrow out of or extricate oneself from an enclosed space, to sing or dance well, to have a strong grasp, to be successful in fishing or hunting, are all believed to be conferred by one or another were-animal, fish, bird, or type."[10] It is interesting to note the similar conception of the source of extraordinary talents or powers in the Romanian village. A villager who has special capacities in finishing arduous tasks, in accumulating money, or as a singer or musician is called a *strigoi pe bani, pe muncă, pe muzică*, etc.; that is, a "witch for money, for work, for music." For these last, as for the witch who steals milk from the village cows or takes the life-force from the fields under cultivation, the origin of such special powers is the magical other world, without the intermediary, necessarily, of a particular were-animal. Nevertheless, the key similarity is the inclusion of "positive" talents that, with maleficent powers, reinforces the wrongdoers' place in society by showing possible alternative commonality with those who may be its leading figures. In Banyang society, moreover, the special brotherhood that does occasionally directly accuse someone specifically of witchcraft, requires prospective members to reveal which were-animals they themselves possess. (p. 346)

The differences between the Dinka, Banyang, and Romanian village models of were-wolves and witches and the wild and savage examples that we are accustomed to see in legends elsewhere in Europe and to view in commercial motion pictures, basically derive from the following: the African societies and Romanian attitudes reflect a balanced approach to social relations. They manifest a desire to permit possible offending members of the community to remain in it, or, alternatively, to maintain the cooperation among and adherence to the social group by all members of the community. The western European models developed from early Christian attempts to suppress witches as emissaries of the devil; to ostracize them or destroy them. We should remember that there was no official religious inquisition in Romania; no organized attempt to eradicate the Romanian community of diabolical figures of malevolence. As we have learned from psychological studies of repressed material such as, in this case witchcraft, the original stimulus unfailingly resurfaces or assumes different forms and beings. Films of vampires or were-wolves, or Dracula, or lately sharks and devil possession, continue to entertain and attract the attention of millions of people, like an infantile complex once more revived or a primitive belief that seems once more to be confirmed.[11]

*   *   *

The wolf has, from ancient epochs, been a symbol of ambivalent cultural values in Romania and in the Indo-European community in general. From the Sanscrit *vricas, varkas*, the Russian *volk* and Serbian *vuk*, the etymological root of wolf is "robber." Compare also the Slovenish *vrag, wrog*, "demon, devil."[12] The ancient Hittite legal concept of serious crime as the breaking of one's bonds with the community led to the definition of the criminal as a "wolf" worthy to be "strangled," to be expulsed from the community.[13] On the other hand, the secret societies of antiquity that put on the skin of the wolf, or were believed to have assumed that animal's form, were, at times, fierce warriors capable of superhuman strength in battle who thereby gained access to the paradise of their gods. The significant feature of this historical image is the reduction of the positive element of the wolf-man in Europe and the subsequent complete emphasis on the criminal, and later satanic, monster.

In the northern European Germanic tradition "wolf" again designated the monstrous criminal and social outcast. From Jacob Grimm to the twentieth century, legal scholarship found that the standard Germanic term for "outlaw," or "peaceless man" was *warg*, Old Norse-Icelandic *vargr*, Old English *wearg*, Medieval Latin *wargus*, and that its basic meaning was "the strangler, the wolf."[14] The Franks put the matter succinctly: "wargus sit hoc est expulsus" ("he is a wolf/criminal, therefore he is expelled"); and the Normans, even more briefly, "Wargus esto" ("Be an outlaw, henceforth"). Similarly, in Anglo-Saxon society, an outlaw or *utlagh*, was said to have the head of a wolf.[15] Such views of the wolf may have had a foundation in the Old Norse-Icelandic myths of Grettir, who "desecrated graves, despoiled corpses, and wrestled with monstrous supernatural enemies," or of Odin, patron of outcasts and leader of the *berserkir*, (literally, "wearing a bear shirt")—"frenzied, shape-changing warriors. . . characterized by insane bloodlust. . . ."[16] And yet, the wolf-warrior represented the most desirable qualities for the defense of the ancient tribes: virility and frenzy in combat and in the hunt; and the patron of warrior societies was quite often as with the Romans, Dacians, Iranians, Scythians, and Mongolians of Gengis-Khan, the wolf. In these peoples, the wolf was conceivably a *natural* model for the qualities they required for life and longevity. As they lived in a closer relationship to the wild fauna, they selected a part of that world for their symbol of protection and aggressiveness.

The great number of ancient Indo-European tribal names that mean "wolf-men" or "she-wolf people" found in Italy, Greece, the Balkan peninsula, Asia Minor, and northwest Iran suggests, furthermore, that the Indo-Europeans shared a common system of beliefs and rituals pertaining to wolves and the assimilation of their carnivorous behavior.[17] Linguistic evidence points to special similarities among the Iranians, Thracians, and Germans. The history of the latter three peoples manifests documented ritual of ecstatic lycanthropy.[18] The transformation into a wolf and the imitation of that animal's ferocity occurred during the warrior ceremonies of secret associations or confederations studied in Indo-European north dieu and still found, as late as the nineteenth century, in Africa's leopard leagues of Liberia, Gabon, and Cameroun. Among the populations that the Greek historian Herodotus called "Scythians" were found the Saka (the name the Iranians gave to the Scythians) Haumavarka, and the Neuri. The first of these tribes used the ecstatic beverage soma as part of the were-wolf rites,[19] and in the second, it was believed that each member of the tribe changed into a wolf for a few days each year.[20] Haumavarka is a combination of "soma" and "wolf"; Iranian in origin – the language adopted by the Scythians after their migration from central Asia to southern Russia and northern Iran. The Iranian *haumavarka* suggests, furthermore, that the custom existed generally in Iran.

The Thracians, ancestors of the Romanians, who were strongly influenced by the Scythian culture, possibly borrowing their vegetation god Zalmoxis from them,[21] included within their nation the Dacian and Getic tribes of the present-day Romanian provinces of Transylvania and Wallachia. "Dacian," as observed by Mircea Eliade, means "wolf people," and possibly may have derived from a culturally borrowed custom of ecstatic lycanthropy. Eliade further speculates that the people who later gave their name to the whole territory of the Thracians north of the Danube may have taken it from a band of fugitives from other regions; that is, from young men living like wolves as they underwent a temporary probation of warrior initiation, or immigrants seeking a new territory to settle, or outlaw refugees who behaved like wolves, but who enjoyed the protection of a wolf-god like Romulus and Remus.[22] The Dacian battle standard showed the image of a dragon with the head of a wolf, which indicated an awareness of the relationship of the wolf and dragon to war.[23] We should note here that the dragon was seemingly another common Dacian figure of military attack and of defense against harm. Although not the object of a formal religious cult, the dragon's image was worn on amulets around the neck or carved on grave markers, in connection with their broadly distributed belief in its protective powers as, for instance, against the evil eye.[24]

In the pre-Christian world, furthermore, in addition to the criminal code, wolves were identified with warfare, death, bravery, and the underworld. Among the Egyptians, for example, Osiris appeared in a wolf's shape to help Horus take revenge on Set.[25] The wolf-god Ap-uat performed the function of psychopomp and was regarded as the son of Osiris who defended him and walked in front of him in ceremonial processions.[26] Similarly, the wolf was the sacred animal of Apollo who, before his identification with Helios and the sun, had been the god of the dead. Again, in the Italian peninsula, among the Etruscan tomb paintings, Hades is clothed in a wolf skin.[27] The Sabines called the priests who served Soranus, their god of the dead, *hirpi*, "wolves."[28] In Greek lycanthropic anthropophagy described by Pausanias, Pliny, and Plato, found in the Peloponnesian Arcadia in the sanctuary on Mount Lyceum dedicated to Zeus Lukaios, those who ate of the human remains of sacrificial victims were transformed into wolves; Pliny believed that the regular observance of this rite underlay a brotherhood of werewolves.[29] This is the general opinion, also, for all the warrior-wolf secret societies from India and Iran to Scandinavia expressed by Jean Przluski, but which is not echoed by Georges Dumézil nor Mircea Eliade.

The *berserkirs* of the Germanic *Ynglingasaga*, it is true, were prey to frenzied bloodlust whether enveloped in the skin of a bear, or as the *ulfedhnar*, men dressed in wolf skins. Through this fury and ferociousness they became the animals themselves: "their furor exteriorized a second being which lived within them."[30] At the same time, the entire process displayed characteristics of initiation into an animal confraternity (preserved in the *Volsunga Saga*), of a shamanic religious experience, for, as in the opinion of Eliade, on the level of religious possession, the beast of prey represents a higher mode of existence.[31] That is to say, the eminent warriors of the Germanic tradition, led by their god Odin, incarnated, in their animal form, a higher religious force, and gained access to the other world, to Valhalla. But even on this side of paradise, a "retired" *berserkir* such as Ulfr, depicted in *Egils saga Skallagramssonar*, was esteemed for his good counsel, enjoyed the welfare he had gathered in his glorious campaigns, and busied himself with his animals and workshops. And, along with his domestic pursuits, in the evening when he often dozed, the rumor traveled that he was still out roaming as a wolf; for which reason he was given the name of kveldulfr, "wolf of the evening."[32]

In sum, in order to explain the persistence and universal dissemination of were-wolf beliefs in an *Indo-European* mythological context, in Mircea Eliade's view, we must look to an ancient religious complex of brotherhoods of wolf-imitating warriors or magicians. More importantly, the unifying element of the belief systems regarding animal incarnations, as they are found in different historical moments among independent cultural models, derives from the "magico-religious experience of solidarity with the wolf, whatever the means used to bring it about: anthropophagy, *furor heroicus*, imitation by putting on the pelt, ceremonial intoxication and rapine and so on."[33]

In any case, in the Middle Ages, the human embodiment of the wolf had ceased to have the socially redeeming role of warrior and protector, and had been limited to the figure of a bloodthirsty, diabolical predator of isolated families and individuals. These settled societies lived as cultivators. To the extent that their identity derived from the regulated flora, rather than war and the hunt, the wolf represented the external menace against which they defended themselves as a group, and an intrusion they sought to foresee and exclude. Thus, the accused were-wolf was beyond the pale, was an outcast, a creature who had forfeited his place in society. Gradually, particularly in southern Russia, Turkey, and Greece, the carrion-eating wolf/were wolf became associated with the undead vampire feeding on the living; both sustained within the concepts of witchcraft, witch familiars, and devil worship. The first operation was very likely a "natural" sort of generalization of functions, particularly in reference to the wolf as lord of the *dead* and psychopomp in Babylonian, Egyptian, and Greek mythology. The second, though, of devil worship, was mainly the responsibility of the developing Christian religion. The Russian *volkodlak* from *volk*, "wolf" and *dlak*, "hair" which originally meant "werewolf" is used today to designate a vampire. The Serbian and Bulgarian *vukodlac*, Czech *vilkodlak* and Greek *vrykolakos* all derive from the root "were-wolf" but again in modern usage mean "vampire." On the outlying Greek islands where the Slavonic influence was weaker, the older Greek terms for vampire still persist.[34] The Romanian *pricolici* is closer to the neutral English term that comes from the Latin *vir*, "man"; its components are *irpu*, "turned in" and *liciu*, "wolf": reversed wolf skin (the hair being worn under the human skin).[35] This correlates with the belief in Romania (as commonly elsewhere) that to make a were-wolf bleed will bring the human spirit to the surface and cause the immediate reversal to the human form.

With the ascendancy of Christianity, the leader of the Scandinavian *berserkir* was reduced to the ogre of the castle on top of Jack's beanstalk, and the lightning-god Thor and the messenger-god Hermes blended with the faun-like Pan into the "grotesque Teutonic devil."[36] Already in Augustine's era the doctrine of the punishment for the sin of Adam was widened to render the human race the "plaything of demons."[37] At the same time magicians were busy persuading their clients that they could turn the latter into wolves with the application of a magic salve.[38] By the fourth and fifth centuries, Roman society was grouped in such a way that the sole practitioners of magic were found outside the Christian community, and the identification of paganism with magic were pervasive: "Men joined the new community to be delivered from the demons; and the new community, in turn, resolved its tensions by projecting them in the form of an even greater demonic menace from outside."[39] At the end of the sixth century, the only remaining outsider in the Christian community, the Jew, began to face the choice of baptism or exile; and the practice of sorcery, gained by a compact with the Devil, no longer permitted the reintegration of the sorcerer into the society despite a promise to recant his knowledge, because he was considered to have completely abandoned his (human) identity, his Christian baptism. (p. 35, 36)

At the close of the twelfth century, and this is deliberately a brief sketch of a centuries-long evolution—my aim is to call attention to the final transformation of the were-wolf from supernatural warrior to supernatural outcast—the last remaining step had been taken. The religious deviant, the heretic and witch became full-fledged worshippers of Satan, and the chronicle of one such instance was recorded in Aquitaine and Burgundy by Walter Map or Mapes, an Englishman living in France.[40]

The Inquisition was founded in France in 1230 and by the fifteenth century, traditional orders were indoctrinated with demonological treatises of scholasticism such that when they came in contact with certain popular traditions of magic and superstition, they used the instruments of trials and punishments against them. In the last years of the fifteenth century, two papal bulls from Innocent VIII, reiterated that the Devil reigned supreme over the world and could claim to his honor its plague of "steaming funeral piles" and "dripping gallows." In the next centuries, the Devil became the sinister "arch-wolf" and was frequently portrayed as a wolf in writings such as Robert Gobin's *Les Loups ravissans ou doctrinal moral* of 1520 and De l'Ancre's *Tableau de l'inconstance des demons* of 1613. The Anglo-Saxons

and Normans also, in medieval texts, represented the Devil as a were-
wolf.[41] And specifically, in 1521, two men from Besançon revealed
that, following a pact with the Devil, they had obtained a salve which
they used to change themselves into wolves. (p. 97) In a later example, a female were-wolf claimed to have snatched a young child from
a river and taken it to Satan who sucked its blood from out the big
toe. (p. 107)

Jean Marx linked the fifteenth century Inquisition in the province
of Dauphine in France to the fact that "they firmly believed that...
the Devil was the director of the blasphemous army of witches...
dedicated to evil and celebrating the sabbath,... When... faced with
a certain stage of magical beliefs and folk superstitions, the encounter
of the abstract dogma of the judges and the concrete reality of the
peasants unleashed the repression."[42]

A particular example of a popular cult of witchcraft that was
directly modified by the pressure of the religious Inquisition in Italy
and thus came to resemble the rites and practices of Devil worship is
described by Carlo Ginzburg. The benandanti, of the late sixteenth
century, were an agrarian cult of wizards who opposed the evil deeds
of witches and cured the victims of the witches' spells; the victory of
their struggles signified an abundant harvest. Failure meant scarcity
and famine.[43] In 1634, after fifty years of Inquisitorial trials, a ben-
andante confessed to Sabbath celebrations of indiscriminate sexual
intercourse, a pact with the Devil, abjuration of Christ and the murder of three children. (p. 133-34) Another prisoner as the judges attested, "confesses everything which is suggested to him." (p. 148)
Thus did an archaic cult of fertility become a black-magical practice
due to the interrogations.

Ernest Jones lists the five main characteristics that together com-
posed the witch/were-wolf heretic of the fifteenth through eighteenth
centuries: incubus, vampire, were-wolf, devil and witch. All had had
an independent existence before the Middle Ages, and continue to
exist periodically in the present day in widespread areas of the world.
For their fusion into a composite belief from the twelfth century onward, the Christian Church and in particular the Roman Catholic
and Greek Orthodox Churches bear, in every case, the prime responsibility. "It was," he concluded, "reserved for the Middle Ages to
plunge into an obscurantism that the so-called Dark Ages had rejected."[44] The formulation of the attitude of the Church was the product of the fear and hate it displayed towards unorthodox worship
which it equated with disobedience against God, and its exaggerated
effort toward sexual repression and a horror of incest. (p. 238)

*   *   *

In the medieval Christian era, therefore, the status of the wolf as
cohort of the gods of the dead and the underworld was projected onto
the new lord of the chthonic realm, the embodiment of evil, Satan.
In this way, the destructive features of the wolf were emphasized,
and particularly its descent from ungodly enemies and dangerous
ogres. Nevertheless, the Romanian body of folk beliefs and legends
that describe the origin and behavior of the were-wolf and witch,
where, parenthetically, the vampire is rejected and universally repul-
sed, seems to maintain the features of pre-Christian, Indo-European
wolf brotherhoods. An example that may make this more clear is
the fifteenth-century Romanian warrior and ruling prince, Vlad
Ţepeş, also known as Dracula because of his father's membership in
the "Order of the Dragon" (drac), founded in 1498 by Sigismund of
Luxembourg, Emperor of Austria and Hungary. The Order of the
Dragon was a brotherhood of martial knights.[45] Dracula is of course
well known to us as the vampire character in Bram Stoker's late-
nineteenth-century novel of the same name. The connection between
Vlad Ţepeş, dragons, vampires, wolves and the Devil occurred in
either Bram Stoker's or the Romanian popular imagination; more
likely the former.[46] Although the medieval bestiaries of western
Europe defined the dragon as the Devil as a matter of doctrine, and
the contemporary Saxons and Hungarians of Transylvania hated and
feared him and carefully chronicled his bloody exploits against his
enemies, still, there are no folk legends that recount the vampiric
machinations of Vlad Ţepeş returned from the grave, persisting in
life through the blood of relatives, enemies, or Englishmen. It is, furthermore, unlikely that Dracula, sworn to defend Christianity against
the infidel Turk invader would emblazon his attire, weapons, and
flags with the dragon if this meant that he was serving in the ranks of
Satan.

The significance of this point is, moreover, that the dragon persisted
as a symbol of Romanian military spirit to the end of the Middle
Ages, at least. And furthermore, my fieldwork to date has shown that
the were-wolf and witch/vampire enjoy a much saner and balanced
treatment in modern Romanian village lore. This is plausibly because
their ancestors' initiation rites in wolf fraternities achieved unity
with a symbol of courage and strength. At least we know that the
Dacians demonstrated an attitude of reverence and respect for images

of the wolf and dragon. And this attitude, lastly, has not been contravened by the might of a religious inquisition, nor the pressure of witch persecutions.

As Jacob Grimm remarked on the popular belief that an encounter with a wolf in Germanic tradition would promise good fortune to the undertaking of bold and brave deeds,[47] there are also further remnants of the Indo-European traditions in the modern world, namely, the attenuated forms of animal incarnation at the time of the winter solstice, the pre-Lenten Carnival, and the spring equinox that may illuminate the magico-religious nature of ancient wolf brotherhoods.

There is first the seasonal characteristic of the martial initiatory rites; in particular beginning with the Scythian Neuri, the periodicity of whose transformations to wolves suggested an annual ceremony. The work of Lily Weiser and Otto Hofler has underscored the relationship between seasonal masquerades of young people wearing costumes of wild animals and specifically those of bears, goats and wolves. R. Bleichsteiner, Octavian Buhociu and Georges Dumézil find that such rites are still current in the Romanian Balkans—and widespread in the west Slavic and Germanic language areas. Most often, the custom is maintained during the ten days from Christmas to Epiphany based on the belief in the periodic return of the dead spirits. Added to this was the rite of initiation of young people into adulthood with ceremonial horse, wolf, goat, and bear masks.[48]

In Romanian village life, these masked and costumed celebrants are very active at this particular time surrounding the new year, and their appearance and behavior does include elements of inflicting fear and diluted "rapine"; the ultimate effect of which, though, is to restore the community. There is a repeated quality of ambivalence in the ceremonies related to the beginning of the new year, and which is present in the căluşari ritual of Pentecost with its animal motifs and theme of animal behavior which I have described in an earlier article,* and in the beliefs and customs surrounding the Sântoaderi where one uses the power of potentially injurious fairies and spirits to reinvigorate and replenish the village. The ambivalence of "helping" fairies, or alternatively, the necessity of carefully channeling chthonic powers that are potentially maleficent or beneficent may explain the tolerant attitudes of respect and precaution in Romania toward the elsewhere normally ostracized and excommunicated were-wolf and witch.

*East European Quarterly, XIV, 3 (Fall, 1980), 303-314.

The Romanian model, finally, differs from other western European attitudes toward the wolf-outcast-criminal in its view that the power underlying them is itself essential to the well-being of the community in general. For example, the *călușari* dancers organize to protect the community from the *iele* in a full natural setting—the stronghold of their adversaries. Or, alternatively, there is the ambivalent nature of the *Sântoaderi* that may inflict severe pain and disfigurement but who also offer gifts and favors if approached with the correct ritual at the proper time. There is, in this way, a fear of the magical beings such as the *pricolici* or *strigoi* who remain marked by the chthonic realm, but who, at the same time, retain a functioning and accepted relationship in the community. The were-wolf and witch enjoy an uninterrupted bond with the community although their co-villagers use precautions in dealing with them and will react with any necessary force if directly endangered. The vampire, of course, has ceased his/her link to life and human society and is universally excluded. It is as if Romania had established a dialectic between the warrior symbol of pre-Christianity and the criminal strangler. In this way, the possible socially beneficial contributions of witches and were-wolves to the community are preserved while their danger is made known and necessary protective measures are prepared.

CHAPTER THREE

ROMANIAN WERE-WOLVES:
SEASONS, RITUAL, CYCLES

From Christmas to Epiphany, confederations of young unmarried men parade through Eastern European villages singing ritual hymns (called *colinde*) and performing dances, accompanied by musicians and others wearing animal masks. The days and weeks before and after Christmas are likewise celebrated in Romania with masquerading, mumming, and folk dramas using masks that represent animals, old people, and devils, in addition to animal costumes. Folk plays called *capra, ursu, călațu, barza,* and *cámila* combine flute playing and dancing with the dramatized bartering, disenchantment from the evil eye, or revival from death of a goat, bear, horse, stork, or camel.

Some were wolf legends[1] attribute enchantment to the conception of the child on the eve of Christmas or Easter, or to birth on Easter. Were-beings appear in the villages on the eve of high religious holidays such as Christmas, New Year's Day and Easter. Christian holidays are likewise the focus of sexual restrictions inscribed in the church canons; that is, one must observe abstinence from sexual relations on the eve of Christmas, Easter, and Pentecost. Failure to do so, and the possible conception of a child will, according to informants, bring deformity and "animal characteristics" to the infant at birth. The victim will be cursed with "wolf ears," for example, or a "wolf's head," or will have a hare lip, and generally will be "unlucky" and even malicious. The legends tell of children who, conceived on the eve of Christmas or Easter in violation of the religious canon, or born on Easter, became were-wolves and harbored resentment and hostility in their hearts against their parents for the latter's transgression. These stories make explicit what exists virtually in the related village beliefs. The period of concomitant witch or vampire behavior is said to begin on the eve of Saint Andrew's feast day (30 November), and extends through Christmas and the New Year to Epiphany.

According to these legends were-wolves and vampires emerge at a specific season of the year. Christmas and the New Year appear to be the primary interlude with Easter and Pentecost as a secondary period. Furthermore, the affiliation of were-wolves with the moon signifies an accessory set of natural cycles. In Roman Jakobson's view, the Slavic were-wolves of Serbia, Bulgaria, Slovenia and Czechoslovakia devour the sun and the moon because they love darkness and to proclaim the triumph of the nocturnal element.[2] Their Romanian cousin, the *vîrcolac*, etymologically "were-wolf," but which has been replaced by *pricolici*, eats the moon. Related also are the Italian and Sicilian traditions of the future were-wolf who was conceived at the new moon, or who slept under a full moon on certain weekdays in summer, or who is stirred to metamorphosis at the full moon, as in numerous European traditions.[3]

The shepherd and goat or gypsy and bear show was at times a simple amusement with the playing of a shepherd's pipe and the dancing of the animal to receive *bacşiş* (gifts, tips)). Other variants added burlesque elements and two new characters, "old man" and "old woman." In its full-fledged form, the actors present a story of the sale, purchase, death, and resuscitation of the animal. That is to say, a merchant first bargains over and then refuses the animal; he is followed by a gypsy who buys the animal, tries to milk it, is angered by it and with a blow to the head, kills it. Either the priest or wise person is summoned, and, reading from a book, or working private magic, recalls it to life. The demand for a reward for the service is the basis of this spectacle's final buffoonery.[4]

The animal folk plays and the custom of masquerading with animal and devil masks are especially prevalent in the provinces of Moldavia, Bucovina (northeast Romania), and northern Transylvania, but exist also in Wallachia and Oltenia (between the Carpathian mountains and the Danube), and are widely identified in the European geographic areas of Slavic and Germanic language concentrations. In Slavic areas, for example, one finds pantomimes with phallic motifs, humorous dialogue, and wolf, bear, horse, aurochs, and goat masks.[5] They are, overall, pastoral ceremonies that, in the minds of many scholars, including Georges Dumézil and Mircea Eliade, reach back to a prechristian belief in the return of the spirits of the dead, of human-animal beings, commemorated by masked figures and animal masks.

My intention in this study is to explore some of the paths of mythological connections between animals, masks, nature, and Romanian village communities. I am not attempting to identify the ultimate origin of the masking games and dramatizations, but rather only to point out that were-wolf legends are merely a part of an entire corpus of ballads and narratives, rites, and customs that describe the interaction of humans and animals, many of which occur in an obviously religious or ritual framework. In this way it will be shown, I believe, that folklore materials can be usefully classified and explained in reference to the context of beliefs, custom and traditional behavior that occur during the interaction of the members of the community in their daily lives, exchanging views and news of familiar events with recognizably common protagonists. Heretofore the task of discovering the meaning and function of were-wolf and vampire legends has generally remained with the psychoanalysts whose analytical methods presuppose their origin in the life history and imaginative projections of individuals in unrelated social contexts and isolated time periods. My effort here is to maintain the theoretical contributions of Arnold van Gennep in his *Manual of French Folklore* and his studies of provincial traditions. In addition, I echo a recent plea from another French folklorist's study of the full range of ritual and belief of Carnival (Claude Gaignebet, *Le Carnaval*) as he argues for increased emphasis on folklore and mythology to interpret a specific set of folk customs and symbols normally given over to psychological interpretation in the absence of surviving mid-winter festivals and mythological rationalizations. I seek, lastly, to furnish a more complete image of the Romanian traditions which integrate magical beings into the villagers' consciousness and make them a part of the surrounding communal setting. Many of the ceremonies of masquerading, animal costumes, and the related legends and beliefs are linked to the season of the year between Christmas and Easter.

The association of Easter with Christmas and New Year in Romania with the conception and birth of a future were-being indicates a larger seasonal period that extends from the winter solstice to the spring equinox. Following Georges Dumézil's study of the horse and wolf motifs in Greek, Indian, and Roman ritual that occurred in the month of February (*Le Problème des centaures*), Claude Gaignebet (with Marie-Claude Florentin) views the contemporary pre-lenten Carnival and its masks, costumes and portrayals of the "grim reaper," as surviving historical composite of animal, religious, and astral beliefs with an Indo-European origin. He speculates that the organization of the Christian calendar developed from a prechristian custom of dividing the year into forty-day periods corresponding to one and one-half phases of the moon with emphasis on the new and full moons. The

key to the establishment of the traditional Carnival was a close obser-
vation of natural patterns; specifically, the dehibernization of the
bear and the attendant beliefs concerning the end or prolongation of
winter. For example, popular tradition in France and Europe tells us
that the bear looks out on February 2 (as the ground-hog in parts of
the United States). If it sees a full moon, it will postpone its final emergence forty days; that is, until the new moon. If, on the contrary, it
sees no moon, it remains out and inaugrates the Carnival period; that
is, the end of winter.[6] Carnival denotes therefore the darkest time at
the end of winter before the renewal of spring. The original initiation
of Carnival at new moon on February 2, "Candlemas Day," the festival light was due to the moon's absence and presupposed a full moon
for Christmas. The early Church had shown an awareness of the importance of the sun by synchronizing the celebration of Christ's birth
with the pre-existing winter solstice. In Gaignebet's scheme, forty-
day periods alternate full moons on Christmas and Easter, with new
moons at Carnival and Ascension (May 1). In conjunction with the
dark moon, furthermore, a modern practice on Candlemas Day is to
prepare pancakes, best exemplified by the Breton style of *crêpes*—
that represent the moon—and eating them to observe its absence from
the sky. (p. 53) It is noteworthy that in Romania, as in eastern Slavic
tradition generally, there is a mythological being that is said to eat
the moon and cause eclipses; in Slavic lore, it is a were-wolf, a *vukodlak*,[7] a term that is confined to "vampire" in modern usage. The Romanian equivalent is a *vîrcolac*, in the past a were-wolf or vampire, but
more commonly now an unbaptized, abandoned infant with a voraci-
cious appetite that has become a sort of woods spirit. In prechristian
Roman and Greek civilizations, February was the month to remember
the dead and welcome animal spirits.

Candlemas Day, as represented by historians of the seventh century
originated as a replacement, in Rome, for the February 15 feast of
the *lupercalia*. At that time, bands of young men of the wolf or goat
confraternities ran through the crowds of spectators in the streets
spreading fear and disorder, and lightly whipping young women with
leather thongs from the hide of sacrificed goats. The goat thongs falling on the women were believed to make them fertile.

February was also the ultimate month of the Roman year, a time
which marked the *Parentalia/Feralia* (February 18-21), the remembrance of the dead. Like the Babylonian feast of all souls, the final
day of the Greek Anthesteria, similarly held in February, the Buddhist
feast of the dead, and the Chinese and Japanese Feast of the Lanterns,

it is a very nearly world-wide custom of setting aside a specific period—at times the last days of the year—to honor the dead. In modern western Europe and America, the holiday to pray for the dead falls in early November, inaugurated by Pope Boniface IV in the seventh century to replace the pagan festival. Our Halloween, and the wearing of witches', goblins', and skeleton costumes by children, maintains the mumming related to spirits and ghosts of the dead of the Greek and Roman celebrations later in the year.[8]

February was generally the month of purification and atonement in Rome, as Ovid's *Calendar of Roman Festivals* reminds us. The term *februa* designated, in the time of the "unshorn fore-fathers," anything used to cleanse one's body. February was therefore the month of Luperci who purified the ground with strips of hide, and of the feralia, the "bearing" of gifts to the dead.[9]

In very early times the Lupercalia cleansed the ancient city on the Palatine whose boundaries had been drawn by Romulus. In all times, however, the luperci struck all whom they met with the strips of the skins of goats, but especially women who offered their hands for the blows. In this way, the women were made fertile and were promised subsequent easy child birth. (p. 390) Further, according to Ovid, the god whom the luperci served was Faunus who, they believed, kept the wolves from the lambs; itself another function of the Lupercalia—in addition to the fertilization of women and the promotion of the growth of crops. *Lupercus* stood for "wolf/goat" and signified the union of the two priestly colleges, the wolves and the goats. (p. 392-393) Moreover, Luperca was the she-wolf that suckled Romulus and Remus, and "februata" or "februaris" is a secondary title of Juno, the patron goddess of marriage. The festival, in conclusion, very likely represented the fertilization and rejuvenation of the community through marriage.[10] Incidentally, in later years, were-wolves were believed to exercise their baneful activities in the month of February, and epidemics of lycanthropy have occurred in the same month.[11]

Thus far we have priestly colleges named the "wolves" and the "goats" who served a woodlands deity that protected the flocks from wolves, the female wolf that had adopted and protected the ancestor heroes of Rome, and a ritual to renew the society and communal lands at the end of winter. Add to this the purification of the city, the festival of the dead and propitiation of the spirits of the deceased, and one begins to see patterns of wolves, the dead, ritual, and fertilization.

The winter months in general, and January and February in particular in Greece, marked the worship of Dionysius, in honor of whom at this time occurred the festival of the Anthesteria. This ceremony, dedicated specifically to Hermes, the guide of the souls of the dead, observed another ritual incidence of their return, and commissioned the populace to offer pots of cooked food to propitiate them.[12] The first day of the Anthesteria, called the Feast of Beakers, meant a beaker of new wine was given to each guest at a public banquet. On the second day, the "Queen" (the wife of the chief magistrate of Athens, that is, the "King"), celebrated her ritual marriage to Diony-sius, and on the third day, the pots of leguminous seeds or cereal were set out.[13] It was customary in the festivals of Dionysius to in-clude natural, "bestial," or lustful merriment. Processions in honor of woodland gods presented dress and behavior in the guise of their companions: Satyrs, Bacchae, and Sileni, "through whom life seem-ed to pass from the god of outward nature into vegetation and the animal world."[14] With the legs of a goat or an ass affixed to a human trunk, their boisterousness, indecent actions and appearance evoked the lupercalian renewal and remembrance of the spirits of the dead.

Mumming and processions did not cease with the disappearance of the ancient gods in Greece. There are today costumed parades that take place during the twelve days of the Christmas season. But in this case, the participants dress up to resemble the monstrous callicantzari that emerges at the dark of the solstice to take control of the world. Modern-day Greek celebrants blacken their faces and cover them-selves with feathers.[15] The callicantzari are pictured as covered with shaggy hair, heads and sexual organs out of proportion to the rest of their body, and legs, ears, and horns borrowed from the goat. (p. 193) Lawson portrays them, moreover, as men "seized with a kind of bes-tial madness which often effects a beast-like alteration in their appear-ance. . . [the victim of which] displays all the savage and lustful pas-sions of a wild animal." (p. 208) Similar to Romanian were-wolf be-liefs, children born on Christmas Day or between Christmas and Epi-phany, in modern Greece, are destined to become callicantzari. (p. 208) And in some areas the term callicantzaro-callicantzari is itself the modern Greek designation for were-wolf.[16]

There are other examples of mid-winter appearances of emissaries from the dead and the underwold as, for instance, the Romanian vil-lages in Macedonia that identify their goblin as the carcandzali,[17] and the Serbs among whom Christmas Eve is an especially dreaded period of were-wolf and vampire behavior.[18] Wilhelm Hertz, in his early but essential catalogue of were-wolf beliefs, reported that in Rus-sian folk traditions, Christmas Eve celebrations included participants in wolf costumes that raced through the onlookers teasing and tormenting them, pursuing them into their yards and houses, snatching up whatever caught their fancy. (p. 122) Svatava Jakobson's description of Slavic folklore supplements the evidence of ritual plays and animal masks, the purpose of which, according to Georges Dumézil, is to dramatize the abrupt appearance of wandering invisible spirits. Accordingly, the masqueraders are "honored and feared at the same time; they cause people to flee and laugh, make men tremble and are showered with oats by the women.[19]

Broadening the context somewhat, Dumézil links the diluted rapine motifs of masked winter solstice rituals to the costumed celebrations, Indo-European in origin, that represented a horse spirit, a leader of souls to the afterworld. Christmas season mummers and modern era hobby-horse performers share a curing and trance function rooted in shamanism,[20] according to E. T. Kirby as well as the mock terrorism and ceremonial kidnapping of women. And this connection in functions moves us forward in the year to the hobby-horse men. The Basque Carnival figure Almazain, the English Morris dancers and the Romanian *călușari* are three well-known hobby-horse ceremonies with additional Italian, French, Spanish, and Portuguese versions, the "proper time" for which Violet Alford and Rodney Gallop consider to be mid-winter.[21] In Romania, the horse-like *sântoaderi* fairies dance on the bodies of those who venture out at night unprotected on the three nights preceding Shrove Tuesday, and bind them with chains, provoking rheumatic pains.[22] Young women, who are particularly frightened of the *sântoaderi* nonetheless bring bread, salt, and nuts to them on Saint Theodore's eve, and in return, obtain thick, healthy hair, full lips and an early marriage.

Mock terrorism was also a part of the stock gestures of the leader of the *călușari* dancers—in particular dashing into the crowd of spectators, pursuing young women, as I observed and filmed the rite twenty-five miles south of Bucharest, in June, 1975. The male confederation began their dancing out beyond an apricot orchard accompanied by a violin and a hammered dulcimer, and then moved to the court in front of the school; thereafter to a crossoads, and finally to a sports playing field where the "war" episode was enacted. The leader wore a miniature carved horse's head and neck suspended from his waist, and had horse's ears planted on his cap. The name of the rite, *căluș*, is believed to derive from the Latin *caballus*, "horse." And the mission of the *călușari* is to protect the community against the injuries and illness inflicted by the *rusalii* fairies while gaining their power for the benefit and health of the village. In accordance with their warlike task, the dancers held a weapon-like baton, and the leader brandished a wooden sword with which he "disciplined" his men and kept the dance movements and the line-ups in correct formation. The masquerading in wolf, horse, or other animal costumes was, in this way, a symbolic reenactment of the emergence of animal forces and the return of dead ancestors molded into a drama of community renewal and protection.

*   *   *

I would like to return again to another practice that I mentioned at the beginning of this study: the performance of folk Christmas carols or ritual hymns called *colinde* by groups of young male singers and dancers. Described by Octavian Buhoviu, this New Year's rite existed in an especially widespread and vigrous form over centuries in southern Transylvania, near Sibiu, adjacent to Yugoslavia in the Banat region of southwestern Transylvania, and from the northeastern province of Bucovina south to the Danube river, until 1914. After the advent of the collective farms and general state planning in agriculture and animal husbandry, between 1948 and 1958, the festivals grew rare and, for the most part, sporadic. The magical function of community renewal in the ceremonies disappeared, and the entire occasion became, under the direction of the mayors and local party secretaries, a spectacle and an entertainment, and a source of local employment.[23] It is, parenthetically, the same fate that has overtaken the *căluşari* dancers who have all but disappeared from the villages. In this latter case, however, the *căluş* has moved to a performing stage in urban centers where the state-sponsored dance contest emphasizes the theatrical and the acrobatic and ignores the communal and ritual traditions. Nevertheless, the performance of *colinde* enjoyed wide adherence until the middle of this century, and, taken in the context of the songs and rites, is related to the general animal beliefs and ancient ritual surrounding the winter solstice.

The unmarried male youth who banded together at Christmas as observed in Dragus, in the south Transylvanian county of Olt in 1932, gathered first on Saint Nicholas' day (December 6) to select their leaders and plan their activities. On the night of Christmas Eve, the fifteen member band went from house to house in the village singing the hymns and, in the following evenings perfoming dances.

The youths stayed together for two weeks in one house.[24] The association included a leader and two assistants, four stewards of food and sustenance, and others to make and bear the flag, and to announce their passage. Besides the singing and dancing, they presented a hunting drama with animal costumes: lions, eagles, horses, stags, rams, and aurochs.

Although it is not apparent from the above, the *colinde* of Romania are very different from the carols of western Europe; a significant proportion, in fact, have nothing to do with the Christian Christmas. The "Miorita," for example, the best known and most frequently encountered, is the story of a shepherd condemned to die by his jealous companions, but who is forewarned by a confiding lamb that reveals the death-plot.[25] Two shepherds from Wallachia (and here I am using the plot summary from Eliade), envious of the third Moldavian's sheep, horses, and dogs, decide to kill him. The latter's favorite lamb lies in misery, refusing to eat, until, in response to his master's concern, it reveals that he will be killed. The shepherd accepts his fate and asks only that he be buried near his sheep and dogs, with shepherd's tools and pipes to catch and sound the wind's music; that the other sheep be told he married a matchless princess of the world. (p. 227-228)

There are over one thousand versions of the song collected from oral tradition, and there are probably an equal number of poems, plays, novels and pictoral adaptations that reiterate the themes in the ballad. Moreover, it is found in every Romanian province: Transylvania, Oltenia, Wallachia, Moldavia, and Bessarabia,* and it circulates in Yugoslavia and Macedonia.[26] The names of the characters, rivers, and mountains together with the style of the spoken language reflect the regions where the versions were recorded.

Although the episode of the clairvoyant lamb is missing from the Transylvanian variant, the motif of the sheep's lament for their murdered shepherd remains, and more importantly, the objects requested for his burial and the cosmic participation of astral bodies and natural formations is included—as in every other province. It is the preponderance of the pantheistic and astral themes that points to Eliade's concept of "cosmic Christianity" underlying Romanian religious folkore. Romanian peasants emphasize the sacrificial role of the Good Shepherd, and, neglecting the historical elements of Christianity, underscore the "liturgical dimension"—that is, the faithful observance of ritual and ceremony. In the "Miorita," Eliade asserts, one finds a

---

* Bessarabia was claimed by the Soviet Union in 1945 and now belongs to it.

"mystical solidarity between man and Nature" that *enables the shepherd to triumph over his fate.*" (p. 254; Eliade's italics).

Is the story of the ewe-lamb a manifestation of a passive "fatalism" on the part of the Romanian people in general? For the shepherd fails to consider even the possibility of resisting. Or, on the contrary, should it be viewed as the acceptance of an unchangeable, decreed event? If one accepts the latter opinion, the shepherd's death is thus a cosmologically-blessed sacrament. In Eliade's eyes, the ballad exemplifies the manner in which the eastern Europeans succeeded in surviving diasters and persecutions. That is, by virtue of their "cosmic Christianity," the Romanians found "the capacity to annul the apparently irremediable consequences of a tragic event by charging them with previously unsuspected values." (p. 255) As such, the "Miorița" represents the profound creative power of the folk spirit. Although I can personally attest that there is a resigned acceptance of the occurrence of were-wolves, witches, and reanimated dead in the village life, it manifests itself as a reasoned acknowledgment of the universal existence of misfortune and individual transgressions, without, for all that, abandoning the principle of resistance and self-defense. A counterweighing folk ideal of rebellion and struggle, however, stems from the legendary figure of the "haiduk," defender of the unprotected against the encroaching outsider.

The solidarity of man and animals is more closely outlined in Buhociu's study of the general content of the *colinde*, and specifically the description of stag and auroch hunts in which the use of milk, blood, and bones of these animals is designed to eliminate hatred and misery while increasing the health and prosperity of the community.[27] Buhociu notes the numerous legends of the reanimation of a dead lamb by the magical power of hidden or scattered sheep bones.[28]

The carols relate the stories of hunts for lions, stags, and aurochs with the assistance of falcons during which dolphins and eagles occasionally appear. Some *colinde* portray the stag and doe as sacrificial animals from which young marriages create their households. As a youthful hunter comes upon a spring where many deer are drinking, a young stag asks him to spare its life: "You have already killed nine of my brothers and I make ten; from their bones you will build your house;. . . cover the walls with their hides; and stain the walls with their blood."[29] In another instance, a deer begs for his life so that it may be transformed back into a man; for nine years and nine days it had lived as a deer because his mother had refused to nurse him at her breast and had thus condemned him to be a wild animal of the forest.[30] One thinks immediately of the same cause recorded for a were-wolf and of a corollary explanation of babies allowed to return to the breast after weaning becoming future wolfmen that I recorded in my fieldwork.

The hunt for the aurochs (*bour*, in Romanian) is based on two main characters and two main themes. There is the carol of the young man fulfilling the conditions for initiation into adulthood and marriage,[31] and of the young woman companion of the aurochs who has fashioned a green or golden swing between the horns of the wild animal and who is regarded as an initiate of higher, cosmic secrets.[32] The auroch, although extinct in Romania since 1627, lives on in the popular imagination through the Christmas hymns; it is portrayed as an especially wild and dangerous beast with supernatural powers. Historical hunts were organized by the ruling princes, and only groups of hunters went in search of it. Similar to the stag hunts, the slaughtered bull furnished bones, blood, and hide for shelter, but, in keeping with its magical aura, its blood was also sufficient to form a lake and its bones to construct a bridge over streams and rivers.[33]

In addition to the extensive *colinde* material describing the stag and aurochs, the discovery and settlement of the province of Moldavia is traced to the origin myth of Prince Dragos. The theme, present in this epic narrative, of the pursuit of a magical animal into strange and marvelous new worlds, is widely disseminated from India and Persia to the Alpine Tyrol, France and Spain, and from the Huns to the Magyars and Romanians in ancient and more recent sources. The list of same and general discussion of the Romanian variant we find again in Mircea Eliade's *Zalmoxis the Vanishing God* (p. 161)

Lastly, three main Romanian myths and two major themes from lyrical folk poetry flow through all facets of the country's culture, from which the principal writers and composers of the learned tradition have drawn their inspiration. They are the story of the ewe-lamb, that we have already discussed, the legend of the construction of the monastery of Argeș ("Mesterul Manole"), and the tales of the *haiduk* or outlaw, leading the struggle against the imposition of a centralized government structure. The battle of the "real country" with the "juridical country," the state-controlled, is viewed by some as a metaphor for the passage from pastoral to modern life.[34] In the mixed folk and learned tradition, the legendary outlaw, often of noble origin, accompanied by his sister or lover Lelea, is endowed with certain features of the *sântoaderi* horse fairies of Saint Theodore's feast day. (p. 305) From folk songs, finally, come the central themes of longing (*dor*) and spleen or anxiety (*urat*). As a composite tableau, and adding the tragic motif from "Manole" of the burial of the architect's wife in one of the walls of the monastery, we find images of struggle and suffering linked to spiritual confidence and cosmic grace.

After viewing the contemporary collections of folktales, poems, and riddles from Transylvania, as well as the Christmas hymns, Octavian Buhociu is convinced that the magical beliefs expressed therein indicate an ancient magical-mystical religion among the pre-Roman Dacians in which the animal realm held a divine status. Human society sought to achieve the "virtue" that its brothers in nature exemplified. Nature was the ideal, Buhociu believes, and the wolf was a quasi-divine symbol of death and leader of souls to the other world.[35] Moreover the remarkable popularity of the animal world in contemporary legends and customs together with the etymology of the Dacian name ("wolf people")[36] and the use of the dragon image on their battle standard are additional evidence of the ceremonial links with the animal world. It is possible, furthermore, that wolf warrior brotherhoods developed in agrarian communities that, having superceded hunting societies, bestowed a magical-mystical status on hunting and warfare, gaining in religion what they had given up in their social and economic system.[37]

Other scholars have traced the relationship between the seasonal incidence of masquerades, the wearing of animal costumes and the belief in were-wolves. Lily Weiser and Otto Hofler make this claim.[38] And Stig Wikander whose work George Widengren later confirmed[39] concluded that the mumming celebrations of India and Iran derived from warrior confederations whose essential elements included a cult of the dead, of demons, and an orgiastic ritual.

In sum, we have noted the belief in Romania that the origin and transformation to a were-wolf is linked to the eve of religious holidays at the winter solstice and vernal equinox, the seasons of the year given over to many kinds of masquerades and folk plays with animal costumes. It is also the time of the year when hymns are sung that invoke the identity of the human and animal realms with ritual designed to renew and restore the village community. The interlude between Christmas and Easter has historically been the time of roaming spirits of animals and the dead, when masking ritual was believed to capture and make available the power of these spirits. There is the additional opinion that were-wolf legends are themselves the remnants of an institution of wolf or bear warrior societies that originated with

Indo-European pastoral peoples. In Romania, where the wolf performed the role of psychopomp, where a hymn of the winter solstice sings of a man's transformation into a stag due to his mother's refusal to nurse him and were-wolf etiological statements cite the same cause, and where masking games and hobby-horse dancers portray fierce animal-like figures and mock ravishment, the were-wolf and vampire possess a familiarity and currency that is as foreign to our culture as our comparable fright-figures are *alien* to us.

The were-wolf legends present stories of wives attacked by husbands, of villagers forced to defend themselves against menacing were-pigs, it is true, but they also describe villagers who continue to reside in the village even after their periodic wolf metamorphosis (or claim to it) is commonly known. Solitary wolves, furthermore, fed by travelers camping in the forest subsequently richly reward their benefactors for shattering the were-wolf enchantment. And if wolves cluster around mysterious human leaders, likewise patron saints of wolves, Peter and Andrew, direct and nurture their animal charges.

Romanian villages offer us, in conclusion, a larger mythological cosmology and context of folk traditions in which were-wolves and vampires find a more natural place.

CHAPTER FOUR

DRACULA

Emily Gerard, whose *The Land Beyond the Forest* probably constituted the richest single source of folklore information for Bram
Stoker's *Dracula*, in the opinion of the annotator of that novel, Leon-
ard Wolf, looked upon the Romanians of Transylvania as an "ardent,
ignorant, and superstitious race"; "less civilized, less educated, and
also less honest" than their Saxon neighbors, but in whom there lay
a "wealth of unraised treasure, of abilities in the raw block, of uncul-
tured talent."[1] Her book is filled with various sorts of cultural snob-
bism, but her major shortcoming, in my view, was the failure to recognize the "treasure" of the Romanians' folk mythology through
which the village and the cosmic world gained a unified set of relationships that effectively prevented the incursion of were-wolf and
vampire legends into the realm of lived reality. That is to say, besides
dramatizing the dangers they posed, the stories and beliefs from Romanian peasants furnished an explanation for these creatures of rapine
and destruction, described their place in the cosmos, and, as we have
seen, the special nature of their existence. The stories and mythology
seem to have preserved the members of the Romanian society from
the urge to put into practice the bloodthirsty brutality that sometimes took place in countries to the West. This is in sharp distinction
to the famous "vampires" and "were-wolves" of western European
history, including the Maréchal de Retz of medieval France, the Hungarian countess Elizabeth Bathory, Peter Kuerten—the "vampire of
Dusseldorf"—John George Haigh, Albert Fish, and others. Their
stories can be found in such studies of were-wolves and vampires as
Robert Eisler's *Man into Wolf*, John Fiske's *Myth and Mythmakers*,
Sabine Baring-Gould's *The Book of Were-Wolves*, Donald Glut's
True Vampires of History, and Hill and Williams's *The Supernatural*
that freely confuse the folk traditions of magic and the dead with
outbreaks of psychotic perversions. In fact, "epidemics" of were-
wolves and vampires bedeviled, so to speak, Europe for centuries;

[38]

mainly the result of the confrontation between Church inquisitors and folk traditions—which were added to the torture and executions for witchcraft. The folklore was regarded as scarcely anything less than heresy. There were, to be sure, the periodic outbreaks of murderous behavior by self-styled "wolf-men/women," but by the end of the sixteenth century the ecclesiastical courts themselves recognized the factor of self delusion in their personal accounts. Chronologically, accusations for lycanthropy occurred first; mass "vampire" behavior occupies a later place in history, specifically in the eighteenth century, stimulated by the flourishing legends and folk beliefs of eastern Europe. Again, the folklore of vampires is, in my view, separate from the living, misguided, driven members of communities who force their sanguine delusions on their neighbors, are arrested, tried, and proven guilty of specified crimes.

The vampire wave peaked in the 1730's in Hungary, Czechoslovakia, and Poland, as recorded in Dom Augustine Calmet's *Dissertation sur les apparitions des anges, des démons et des esprits et sur les revenants et vampires de Hongrie. de Bohème, de Moravie et de Silésie* that was published in 1746 in Paris. Calmet produced a compendium of legends, newspaper accounts, anecdotes, and letters of firsthand information from friends. Although the survey makes only a brief passing reference to "Walachia," and in particular to the city of Timișoara in western Romania, Calmet's sources of popular traditions were genuine, as later collections have verified. Nevertheless, his attempt to scientifically or theologically authenticate their existence were mere personal speculations. It is extremely important, however, from a folklorist's point of view, that this eighteenth-century catalogue of vampire lore makes no reference to the Hungarian Elizabeth Bathory (1560-1614) who killed young women and children in order to bathe in their blood and preserve her own youth. The countess Bathory is a leading figure in the lists of "true" vampires that star in the attempts to establish the credibility of folk legends. Bathory, de Retz, Kuerten, Haigh, Fish and the rest were neither vampires—they were not dead people who returned to torment surviving members of their families—nor were-wolves: they did not change into an animal form. Peaceless maniacs and convicted criminals, they are related to the Jack-The-Rippers of history, but their behavior has little to do with folklore in general and Romanian traditions in particular. They were fixated on blood; with an erotic blood lust, a *haemotodipsia*; individuals whose "whole sexual satisfaction comes from blood."[2] The blood fixation is at best partially relevant to Romanian legends.

The impulse to change into a wolf or to return from the grave, in the legends I have collected and recorded from published sources, is due, respectively, to the failure to bring the infant and child completely into the human realm (from Nature and the Underworld), or to persuade an adult to abandon his contacts with it at the end of his life. A were-wolf in Romanian lore attacks sheep because it is hungry, or people with whom it has quarreled; a vampire refuses to let go of the world. It seeks to maintain its existence in the community by stealing food or blood; that is, the life essence, from others. It wreaks destruction on the living, or comes back from the grave to assist and watch over surviving relatives. There is a sexual motif that I noted in the work of a collection of folk beliefs from 1945 by Marcel Olinescu which states that a woman vampire will suck the blood from the throat of a man with whom she has had sexual intercourse; leaving her mark there. That, however, represents one trait in an entire network of causative and behavioral motifs; and it may equally well signify the attempt to participate in human existence in a normal way, that is, by making love, while seeking to prolong an in-fact abnormal existence with the blood of the living.

A story that illustrates the way in which a vampire views her relationship to life from the far side of the grave comes from Sălaj in the county of Bihor. In it a young woman returns from the dead, and, among other things, visits her erstwhile suitor; she in the form of a wolf; he while working in the fields. Frightened, he inflicts severe injuries on the wolf to the extent, as she complains later to him, that she is henceforth "less than a woman." (That is to say, unable to bear children.) There are legends of other vampires who cohabit with their living wives after death, and beget more children. The lesson of vampire creatures in Romania is that there are people who are wrenched from life before they are ready to give it up; that is, who die a violent, sudden death. Or, there are others, who commit suicide, whose relationship with life is no less unresolved. And finally, there are those who die without benefit of the ceremonies of the Church, and who therefore wander between life and the other world, unable to enter the latter.

In the same manner that we must look to the historical annals of countries west of Romania for the pathological "vampire" impersonators, we are also able to find there the lists of the hundreds, perhaps thousands of deluded victims and tortured pawns executed for devil worship and "lycanthropy" from the fifteenth to the nineteenth centuries. Although Maria Theresa, Empress of Austria and Hungary, dispatched a commission to Wallachia in 1756 to investigate a vampire panic and reassure the populace,[3] it must be said that Romanian folk mythology restricted its ferocious creatures to legend and narrative; so too did it protect individuals from the unrestrained zeal of religious orthodoxy. Religion in Romania has traditionally been perceived as a corpus of ritual acts and rules for communal ceremonies which, in Mircea Eliade's words, emphasizes the liturgical over the doctrinal, and integrates the baptismal, marriage, and burial rites into other pre-Christian folk traditions.

In like manner, the "vampyrs" of Byron, Goethe, Nodier, Poe and Baudelaire, and the Draculas of Stoker and western films derive from the literary and philosophical contexts of romanticism and decadent Marquis-de-Sadism. This is not to pass judgment on them; rather, only to point out that they belong to a different intellectual and social context. That is to say, even though they are represented as a part of folklore, they owe their characteristics to an academic and literary tradition; to a failure of religious faith and of humanism, and to a revolt against the scientific dogma of positivism and materialism. Authors and protagonists typically portray the outsider, the unintegrated held responsible for the unexplained and the uncanny.

Radu Florescu and Raymond McNally's biography of Vlad Țepeș, the prince of Romania and ruler of Transylvania, known to us as Dracula, while it rehabilitates his reputation in historical annals, implies, by the same token, that Bram Stoker's model of the vampire Dracula was not widely different from Romanian traditions and society. Florescu and McNally discuss the syndrome of erotic blood lust in relation to Stoker's protagonist and imply that the condition is a general feature of vampires from the folk tradition. This is disproved by my research. Secondly, they insist on the "inextricable" connection between folk vampires and the Devil.[4] Agnes Murgoci's work refuted that notion in 1929, and my collection has substantiated her findings that the undead were impelled by nothing but their own souls. And finally, Florescu and McNally assert that the large number of terms used to denote the "various species" of vampires in Romania testify to the prominence of that creature in the minds of the inhabitants, and show the closeness of their similarities to the fictional Dracula. They cite seven terms; three of them, according to my informants and bibliographic sources, have nothing to do with vampires. The *iele* they call "a collection of nasty female vampires"; *iele* are rather mythological female fairies. The *sburător* and *zmeu* are ogre characters and dragons in Romanian fairy tales, the antagonists of

"Prince Charming." They identify the *pricolici* as a species of the living dead who rises from his grave at night in the form of a man or of a wolf or dog" (p. 168); the greater than one hundred legends of *pricolici, tricolici* and *strigoi de lup* in my field collection always identify that human wolf, dog, or pig as a living member of the community, and carefully distinguish his wolf-like behavior from the milk-stealing habits of the *strigoi mort* ("vampire"). Forescu and McNally call the *vîrcolac* a were-wolf, as if that were synonymous with vampire, but whatever the truth of that confusion, and it appears that it signified both in previous years, my informants didn't know the term generally, and two villagers and a folklorist who chose to, defined it as an unbaptized and abandoned infant who causes eclipses by "eating" the sun or moon. That leaves two remaining terms: *strigoi* (female: *strigoaica*), and *moroi* (female: *moroaica*). The latter term, according to an unpublished manuscript on Romanian mythology in Bucharest,[5] is more current in Sub-Carpathian Romania. My point is that Romanian mythology is, at the same time, more complex and contains finer distinctions that Florescu and McNally describe in their biography.

There is no doubt that Bram Stoker made dramatic use of some authentic traditions from Romania and elsewhere. The association of wolves with the vampire, the light specks that signal his arrival, and the lore of Saint George's feast day, April 23, are examples of popular beliefs. Count Dracula, on the other hand, as the immortal bloodsucker who preys on aristocratic English families, is, of course, the product of the author's own fantasy, and judging from the popularity of the novel, his genius.

Nevertheless, there are no legends from Romania, Hungary, Yugoslavia, or Poland that portray Vlad Ţepeş as a vampire returned from the grave. The tales that describe his unrivaled cruelty are found in German and Slavic manuscripts which emphasize the identification of Dracula-Devil, and Romanian narratives that repeat some of the tales, but underline, moreover, in addition to the cruelty of his punishments, the justice of many of his decisions.

Dracula was also known for an illustrious victory in battle, against far superior forces in 1462, over the imperial Turkish army that had come to subjugate the Wallachian and Moldavian principalities (that comprised the territory of Romania in the fifteenth century), and add them to their conquests of Bulgaria and Serbia. Vlad-Dracula accomplished his victory by guerrilla tactics of periodic military attack, destruction of the agricultural infra-structure, evacuating villages, and demolishing bridges before the advancing Turkish army. A local prince with a band of marauders stymied an imperial army that had toppled Constantinople and the Byzantine empire. The events of this era represented a turning point in world history when "a millenium-old empire, the Byzantine, disappeared and the new one, the Ottoman, hadn't yet found its place and assumed the equilibrating factor."[6] Thus, a peculiar set of historical circumstances, in addition to the common-place assassinations, bloody family vendettas, and struggles to mount and hold ruling thrones, propelled Vlad-Dracula into the annals of history, legend, and devil lore.

After the death of his grandfather, Mircea the Old, in 1418, the two main branches of Dracula's family, represented by his father Vlad Dracul and his uncle Dan I, competed for the throne of the Wallachian principality. Romania at this time consisted of the separate provinces of Wallachia, including southern and south-eastern Transylvania, and Moldavia, both of which were fiefdoms to the Austro-Hungarian Empire that directly ruled the remainder of Transylvania. The three traditional areas of Romania were united as one country for the first time briefly in 1600 by Michael the Brave. They were re-united in 1917.

Vlad Dracul, Dracula's father, lost his throne and his life while his son served as a family hostage to the Turks. Dracula captured the crown briefly in 1448 from his cousin Vladislav II with the help of the Turks who viewed him as potentially more favorable to their national interests. Although driven from power almost immediately by Vladislav, himself supported by Iancu of Hunedoara, the Governor of Hungary, Dracula was again a strong contender for the throne eight years later. In this latter instance, Iancu of Hunedoara had thrown his influence behind Dracula; Iancu had grown dissatisfied with Vladislav II's failure to maintain strict opposition to Ottoman Turkey. Very likely as a result, Vladislav was assassinated in the same year at Tîrgisor. The Dracula-Iancu entente was short-lived, however, due to Dracula's subsequent decision to pay the tribute demanded by the Turks. The Hungarians sent Dan II, son of Vladislav II and a rival contender for the throne, to the northern border of Wallachia to undertake his personal quest for the crown. Furthermore, Dracula's tariff and commercial policies had stirred up Saxon traders in southern and south-eastern Transylvania who received Dan II and harbored numerous other pretenders to the Wallachian throne. Dracula responded by arresting and impaling a number of Saxon traders. In 1460, a new agreement with Mathias Corvin, successor to Iancu of

Hunedoara, finances and fervor for an anti-Turkish crusade emanating
from Venice and the Holy See, led Dracula to refuse to pay his tribute
to Turkey. This decision was the cause of the battle and subsequent
historic victory by Vlad-Dracula in 1462. The next diplomatic twist
came from Hungary, which, needing to pacify Turkey while Mathias
Corvin pursued his claim to the Austro-Hungarian title of emperor,
ordered Vlad-Dracula's arrest and imprisoned him for twelve years.
When he was released from prison in 1474, Dracula again waged war
upon the encroaching Turks. He was assassinated by a probable Turkish agent in 1476 while viewing the progress of a battle.[7]

The legends that carried Dracula's fame and infamy East and West
are found in two manuscripts. The first, in German, was found in the
Saint Gall Monastery in Switzerland; the second, in Russian, was discovered in Leningrad. Both texts are reproduced in translation, together with the Romanian narratives in McNally and Florescu's *In
Search of Dracula*, pages 192-208.[8] Of the thirty-two incidents in the
German manuscript and the nineteen tales in the Slavic text, McNally
and Florescu claim four are confirmed by independent sources. They
are: the impaling of Saxon merchants, the murder by arson of a room-
ful of foreigners that had come to Romania to learn the language, the
relocation and subsequent impalement of an entire rich landowner's
family, and the driving of nails into the heads of recalcitrant Turkish
ambassadors to permanently fix the caps in place that they had refused
to remove in the presence of Dracula. Twelve tales are included with
their variants from Romania, six of which are related to the German
and Slavic texts. The remaining narrate stories of dishonest merchants
who attempt to cheat honest but poor peasants and the punishment
the former suffer from Prince Dracula, of Dracula's hatred for Turkish tax collectors who seized herds of sheep and forced Romanian
youths into service in the Turkish army, of wealthy landowners who
conspired with foreigners and who thereafter were impaled, and finally, of the harsh punishment Vlad bestowed on liars, thieves, or those
who behaved badly towards the elderly or who oppressed the poor;
hanging and impalement. (p. 202-208)

In the popular western mind Dracula is identified with "vampire"
and "devil." The term *drac* in Romanian does signify "devil," and
the dragons that adorned the family coat of arms, that were sculpted
on the monastery at Curtea de Argeş, minted on coins of the territory,
and decorated their clothing were widely connected with the Devil
in medieval bestiaries. We have only to recall the very popular legend
of Saint George slaying the dragon and freeing the land from its curse.

The question remains, why would one who proclaimed his undying opposition to the Turks and who joined the Christian crusade against the infidel Ottomans advertise himself as a servant of the Devil and fix the insignia of the Master of Evil to his clothing and coat of arms?

Dracula bore the name of heir to his father Vlad Dracul. More precisely *Drăculea*, "belonging to the Dracul line," "son of Dracul," constituted a sobriquet applied to other members of the family as well, in particular to Dracula's brother, Radu the Fair, referred to in Byzantine sources as *Drăculea cel tînăr*, "Dracula the Younger."[9] An earlier study of Vlad-Dracula describes the form *drăculea* as belonging to oral tradition, with *dracula* the literary and scribal version which appears exclusively in monastic scripts and recorded narratives.[10] Apparently, the name *dracul* arose from two unrelated sources: the first was Dracula's father, Vlad Dracul's reception in 1431 into the "Order of the Dragon" founded in 1408 by Sigismund of Luxembourg, Emperor of Austria and Hungary. The blazon of the order showed a dragon at the foot of a cross; the members wore a green cloak (the color of the dragon) over a red one (the color of sacrifice and martyrdom).[11] The dragon, in contrast to the age's bestiaries, seems to have symbolized invincible bravery, in this instance, rather than the Devil. In any case, the sculpture on the Adomirea Maicii Domnului Monastery of Curtea de Argeş showed the dragon mastering another powerful and fabulous beast with a serpent's head that represented the Turkish foe.[12] Second, the Romanian-origin inhabitants of northwest Transylvania, in the Apusenian mountains, bestowed the epithet "draguli" or "draculi" (the plural of *dracul*) on their brothers from Wallachia, in the same manner that Moldavians were christened "dani" (the plural of *dan*).[13] Vlad-Dracula had himself adopted the appelation by 1475 when his signature read: "Wladislaus Dragwlya, Vaivoda partium Transalpinarium" (Vlad Draculea, Prince of the Transalpine Province).[14] The dragon, in this usage and in the general folklore of Romania as early as the Dacians, did not signify "Satan." To the Saxon communities or to the families of merchants who suffered impalement because of Dracula, the name, on the contrary, very likely denoted a cruel, Satan-dominated ruler. Thus, at a particular moment, in a particular region of Romania, the name gained a decidedly evil cast which was transmitted into other countries of Europe.

CHAPTER FIVE

ROMANIAN FOLK MYTHOLOGY:
DRACULA HAS GONE WEST

Romanian sociologists, in the first years of this century, decried the gap in understanding between the country's urbanized leaders and its rural culture. Dumitri Gusti, the founder of the Romanian school of sociology, in describing the conditions that led to its inception, remarked that foremost was a reaction to the distance between the government leaders' commitment to a "western state" into which they sought to transform Romania, and the "social unreality" of village communities.[1] The attempt to modernize the latter without an intimate comprehension of the peasants' customs and beliefs betrayed their ideal and instilled a stubborn refusal to cooperate in the latter. (p. 4) The primary efforts before Gusti's fieldwork were the nineteenth-century collections of rural traditions that focused on folk tales, lyrical poetry and ballads. And the less frequent compendiums of ritual, magic, and superstition by Simion Florian Marian (*Sărbătorile la Români*, 1889), B. P. Hașdeu (*Etymologicum Magnum Romaniae*, 1886) and Tudor Pamfile (*Mitologie Românească*, 1916), remained, for the most part, isolated data lacking the meaningful context of village life. To achieve a better understanding of rural life, therefore, teams of social scientists devoted their summers to case studies of particular villages. After 1925, geographers, anthropologists, biologists, and hygienists, in addition to the sociologists came together in the "Social units of our country that stood in greatest need of social reform." (p. 7) The Social Service Act of 1938 marked the national recognition of their attempts and created the Romanian Sociological Institute in the University of Bucharest. Numerous published village monographs resulted from the studies in the villages of Nerej (district of Putna), Drăgus (Făgăraș), Clopotiva (Hațeg), and Șanț (Năsăud) among others, by Henri Stahl (1939), Ion Conea (1940), Traian Herseni (1944), and Ion Ionica (1944).[2] These attempts were, in Gheorghe Pavelescu's opinion, in 1941, important steps to penetrate the magic-based "vision" of the world held by the peasants, and with it, the intimate structure of the villagers' view of life as he himself had recorded it in northewestern Transylvania, in the Apusenian Mountains.[3] After the Second World War, professional investigations of village society continued briefly, but then abruptly disappeared. The work ceased after approximately forty studies from 1945 through 1947, and remained suspended until 1958.[4] This was due in part to the deficiencies in Gusti's methodology which called for an "endless collection of material," a mass of indigestible facts that prevented the interpretation and recomposition of the data into a concluding synthesis. (p. 22) And in part it was due to the sharp struggles of differing theories and ideas within sociology. In addition, the agrarian reform and collectivization that began in 1949 brought structural changes to the communities themselves. And the discontinuance of the discipline of sociology itself in the universities between 1948 and 1966 was the final blow. (p. 37) In 1958, however, the village monograph reappeared but with an emphasis on the economics and technology of the state collective farms. Finally, in the late sixties a renewed interest in sociological research in village communities emerged that focused on social change in the context of collectivization, industrialization and the communist regime. Three monographs are particularly representative of the new approaches: Mihail Cernea et al., Două sate. Structuri social și progres tehnic; O. Badina et al., Buciumi, un sat din țara de sub munte, and Nicolae Dunăre, Țara Bîrsei, forthcoming volumes two and four of which treat peasant households and settlements, folk art, customs and intra-family relations. It is only in the decade of the seventies that the renewed sociological focus has once more attempted to define and understand peasant household life and arts, and with these, one would hope, the villagers' Weltanschauung.

In the forties, nonetheless, for Pavelescu and others, notably Ștefania Cristescu-Golopenția in the village of Drăguș, folk traditions constituted a spiritual technology allied to and supporting the physical and economic knowledge possessed by the community. They sought to describe the organized set of material and spiritual concepts through which the country people viewed their world, and underlined the contribution of magic, superstition,[5] custom, and religious thought to that structure.[6] The basic function of the folk technology was to align the people, animals, and activities of the community with the invisible forces that were thought to govern the world.[7] Christian religious beliefs are themselves included in this folk mythology as an assemblage of rites that have proved their applicability and appropriateness through the ages. The Orthodox faith, for instance, continues to be regarded as an historically honored set of rules that merge into the total framework of popular lore, rather than as an abstract and rigid dogma. In relation to wolves, were-wolves and witches, for example, religion furnishes the cosmological foundation that integrates them into the cycles of regeneration and destruction and into the hierarchy of the creation from plants and insects to the saints and God. It is, in many ways, a medieval image of the world in which all living things and creatures have their place and their patron saint, but in which the Devil, although a force of suffering and punishment, is not an every-day participant in the community's world. The entire complex of beliefs is, moreover, shared by and exchanged among the entire village; it constitutes, by itself, the basis for the solidarity of the society that confronts the immaterial forces of existence. All the people of the town, young and old, men and women, identify the supernatural beings that make up their legends and myths in the same language and with similar images. (p. 22)

My research and fieldwork has provided evidence that the above discussion is valid for other areas of Transylvania, Bucovina and northern Moldavia in small villages devoted to traditional occupations such as individual and collective farming, sheepherding, and the preparation of wool. The most striking characteristic of the legends of were-wolves, witches and vampires generally in Romanian folklore is the nearly total lack of Christianization, or rather demonization of the protagonists. In contrast to other European traditions of pacts with Satan, or the theme of expiation of sin through the transformation into a wolf or periodic pilgrimages, Romanian tradition integrates the existence of such monsters into the play of opposing forces between human society, nature, and the underworld/world of the dead. Agnes Murgoci observed in 1935 that "although in Romanian folklore vampires and devils are nearly akin I have found no instance in which the dead corpse is supposed to be reanimated by a devil and not by its own soul."[8] This is not to say that the Devil, in his Christian characterization, is absent from modern-day Romanian folk mythology, but, that his independently forceful powers over individuals are attenuated by the relationship of other elements in the human and natural world. The creation myth in Romanian folklore portrays the Devil as the dynamic collaborator to the "science" possessed by God. The Devil, in God's name, but not without some repeated insistence on the latter's part, dives through the primordial waters and returns with some meager lump of dirt out of which the world is fashioned. It is fitting that the creature given domination over the underworld be assigned the task of fetching a little deeply buried earth for the creation; in Romanian terms, this collaboration demonstrated the necessity of even the Devil to the cosmos. Just as there is misfortune and suffering in life, evil, that is the source of suffering, is an indisputable fact, and the Devil is a necessary antagonist. In this way, he is raised from the depths of his proclivity to sadistic cruelty and devastation to the level of co-producer of the divine creation, and God descends somewhat, in the mind of the peasant, to a more humanized level.[9] Such attitudes as these in contemporary Romanian folklore manifest, I believe, remnants of custom and beliefs of its Dacian ancestors.

The most significant religious belief inherited from the Thracians, the parent race of the Geto Dacians, was the cult of the dead and the belief in immortality. As the earth cycle of vegetation, rebirth, and seasons, so too the existence that continued after death in the underworld was guided by the chthonic Dionysos-Sabazios.[10] The Thracians affirmed the same desire and needs with the potential for good or evil in those gone beyond as in the living. The soul did not, they believed, leave the body; the latter only lost the ability of movement, but preserved the same sentiments and aspirations as in life. (p. 2) An associated but not necessarily chthonic divinity, the Getan Zalmoxis, as described in Herodotus, provides another aspect of this assumption of life after death. According to Herodotus's account (4. 94-96), the disciples of Zalmoxis went to him after death in a place where they would live forever and have all good things (pp. 94 and 96). There is no mention of the soul departing the body, rather the dead would continue to enjoy an existence in the flesh.[11] A related popular animal cult of the same period among the Dacians was the devotion to the serpent-dragon revered for its protective powers against misfortune and witchcraft and which appeared, with the head of a wolf or dog, on the Dacian battle standards depicted on Trajan's column.[12] Nour attests that the serpent was not the object of a formal religious cult, but enjoyed the widest distribution in Dacia in the form of a folk superstition.[13] The significance of serpents and dragons, as opposed to the other animals sacred to the Geto-Dacians, namely the horse, the ox, the ram, and the bull, is their emphatically chthonic origin and habitat. The dragon emerged from the underworld; the land given over to Satan in normal Christian tradition. The Thracian spirituality, a thriving tradition and yet hospitable receptacle for the succeeding Christian culture,[14] by itself accounts, in large measure according to Papadima, for the gravity and solemnity that accompanied all social, magical and religious ritual in contemporary Romanian folklore; for each act and thought creates an effect "on the other side," in the other world. There is, in fact, in popular belief, a basic series of correspondances between the two worlds that is fundamental to the widely held prestablished harmony of the cosmos.[15]

Some of the material in the foregoing and following discussion was recorded in years past, even in the past century, and may have evolved or perhaps disappeared from present-day Romania. Particular groups of belief statements and versions of the legends are village-specific. Certainly, the legends of witches, vampires and were-wolves, judging by the comments of earlier folklorists, have changed. But the fundamental structure and basic worldview of the legends, beliefs, and ritual actions, based on a composite whole, has remained constant over periods of centuries—in the same way that the Romanian language was maintained and survived in isolated mountain villages and on the highly traveled plains alike during the rule and domination of Turkish, Slavic, and Austro-Hungarian migrations and invasions. Many elements of folk beliefs and narratives have undoubtedly been borrowed from conquering and migrating peoples—as have linguistic forms and social customs. A broader comparative study is needed to survey the entire area of eastern Europe to see how each national collection of popular traditions creates a particular and original pattern. I will try to indicate in Chapter Five, as I have done already, where the lore is similar.

With the above in mind, the first fact of Romanian folklore to emphasize is the belief in the existence of the magical powers in the other world, the realm of fairies and of the dead, and the effort to utilize those magical powers for the benefit of the community, while, at the same time, protecting the social group from the harmful effects such interaction with the other world might create. The folk mythology affirms the existence of means of communication between human society and the magical world while it seeks to maintain the essential values and basic norms of human society. It is organized around five or six figures: the *ursitoare*, or three fates, the *iele, zîne,* or *rusalii,* nature fairies, *Mama pădurii,* a woods fairy, the *şolomanar,* sorcerer of rain and tempests, *pricolici,* and *strigoi.* These beings are related to four main life events and community places: the forest or Nature, birth, calendar events, and death.

A second basic character of this mythology is the inclusiveness of its approach to the world and the cohesiveness of its cosmology. All creatures, beings, phenomena from ants to wolves to people and villages have their patron saint and protector, and each has its role and function to perform in the world. The result of such rural attitudes toward, in particular, rapacious animals and the Devil is that the concept of evil is not ascribed to one limited figure or source. Misfortune and suffering do exist, but they are not the products of any particular being solely, but are potentially present in everyone's behavior.

Often, a common source of danger or misfortune may also bring assistance, health and revivification to a community. The *rusalii* fairies threaten to injure and disfigure those who fail to respect their sacred days after Pentecost, but also promise health and well-being to the entire community through the intermediary of the *căluşari* dancers. The horse-like *Sântoaderi* (mythological beings based on Saint Theodore) are the terror of young girls, and may bind their victims with chains and provoke rheumatic pains; they also bestow gifts of beautiful hair and sweet lips to nubile maidens.[16] Dead *strigoi* or vampires that return from the dead may do so, in addition to murdering, raising dins in the attic, or scattering farm animals, to care for their surviving children, to bring food or chop wood for the living. And November 30, the feast day of Saint Andrew, one of the patrons of wolves, the first called of the apostles and thought to be the donor of garlic,[17] is the most propitious time of the year for witches, ghosts and wolves.

The villagers in Romania make sharp distinctions between the symbolic space of the village and forest; between human society and uncontrolled nature. The forest is the residence of wild and threatening animals, for example, bears, wolves, lynx, wild goats, and wild boars, but also, in cosmological terms is the intermediary space between the village—the world of human culture—and the underworld. Sometimes, people bear the mark of the chthonic realm; that is, they are born with the caul, possess a tail ("an extension of the spinal column") or horses' hooves, and wear the stigma of, or alternatively, make use of, the magical power of that place. This is true for cases of great talent or accomplishment or intelligence as well as were-wolves and witchcraft. Nature and the forest is often the place where magic is sought; where contact with the powers of fairies and the dead takes place. Were-wolves run off to the forest when they feel the onset of the spell that makes them change their shape. The *şolomanar* or wizard of lightning and hail-storms, seeks the dragon he will ride through the skies in the mountain lakes, and the *căluş* ritual at Pentecost, as I witnessed it in 1975, began in a full natural setting and thereafter moved to the village center. Finally, the costumes and folk drama that mark the Christmas and New Year's holidays utilize animal figures to commemorate the magical relationship to animals that is celebrated in holiday carols.

The greatest number of magical beliefs are related to birth, which is considered the single most important event in one's life.[18] This is the result of the conviction that the personality is formed in the first days after birth and the entire fabric of one's destiny is woven at this time; a tradition personified in the *ursitoare*, the three divinities that gather around the newly born and prophesy or even determine his or her fate. In some areas, food gifts are set out, the first night after birth for the goddesses, in order to mollify or placate them. The *ursitoare* may confer a particular future on a child by marking him with the caul or a tail, signifying a special talent or an unfortunate predisposition. There is a quite common legend in which the birth goddesses predict a particular child will fall down a well at age twelve and die. The significance of the legend is that there is no escaping the destiny set forth. We have a special relationship to that story because of our daughter's accident in the village of Şanţ where we stayed for one week. The first morning after our arrival, we left our two children at the house of our hosts to drive to a nearby town for food provisions. When we returned two hours later, our hostess came running out to the road crying "mort, mort!" (dead, dead!). Our daughter had plunged head first down the well in the front yard of the house, about twenty-one feet deep, had been cranked back up and was bruised, scratched and terror-stricken, but standing in the bedroom of the house very much alive. Our hosts automatically associated wells and children with death.

The magical time after birth extends, in some instances, up to seven weeks. (p. 43) A new mother must touch nothing for three days until blessed by the priest, lest the child be damned, in the opinion of one Moldavian. Generally, four of my informants asserted that to be born on Easter, Christmas or Pentecost is to be blessed by God;[19] as distinguished from the two legends of children become were-wolves *conceived* on the eve of Christmas or Easter and the one were-wolf born on Easter.

We have spoken earlier of the significance of the Christmas, New Year's and Easter holidays in relation to the traditions of animal costumes, dramatizations, and to the appearance of were-wolves, ghosts, and vampires. The Romanian calendar marks a general succession of good and bad days for the success of a particular activity, and the holidays signal the critical dates of the year.[20] The hours of the day are likewise distinguished according to auspicious or deleterious moments. Especially critical is the time after midnight until the crowing of the cock, for then all manner of baneful spirits are at large. At night, every event has a double significance related to physical laws and to the magical or spirit world, in which the latter interpretation tends to prevail (p. 33). Romanian folk tradition has broadened the calendar of the Christmas and Easter seasons to include the feast days of Saints Andrew, Peter (January 16) and George (April 23). On the eve of Saint Andrew's, it is thought that the animals speak and that the sky opens for the just to see heaven.[21] For some, midway between Easter and Pentecost, branches of blackberry, bramblebush or lovage are hung outside above the doors to the house and animal sheds to guard against *strigoi*;[22] the time of the year normally reserved for the *rusalii*. Saints Peter and Andrew are also believed to send wolves to punish those who fail to respect their feast days by sweeping the floors, eating meat, throwing the garbage out the door, weaving or working, or simply by using a comb or carrying it out of doors.[23] Presumably each of these actions would disturb the saints or possibly spirits of the dead that might be circulating outside the houses; combing one's hair was explained as an action that has no place on a day dedicated to the forest and wild animals.[24] Saint Andrew is also considered a patron of wolves, as are, at times, Saint Nicholas and Dumitru, but the feast day of Andrew and somewhat less frequently Saint George is the time of the year when wolves, witches, spirits of the dead and the undead are the most active.[25]

All of the preceding gives proof of the wide scope and significance that are attributed to religious holidays and saints' days in Romania. But if that were not enough, we should also remember that the important religious holidays are likewise an occasion for honoring and praying for the dead. The week following Pentecost is also called the week of the dead, but on Ascension Thursday as Pentecost, bread, eggs, cakes and wine are brought to the church as offerings for the dead (*pomana*); lighted candles are placed on the bread and cakes, during the service, and all is distributed freely to everyone present, including travelers and the poor at the conclusion of the mass. At this time of the year, the priest often reads all the names of the deceased from the village. This distribution of alms and gifts is thought to honor the dead and celebrate the fruits of life.

The numerous annual days of prayer and remembrance for the dead throughout the year indicate the central place they hold in the villagers' minds. Another indication is the large number of church services and requiem masses said for each deceased person. The first occurs after three days, then at nine days after death, again at twenty days; a requiem mass is said after forty days (after which time the dead are thought to pass over to the other world), and again after six months and a year. At the end of seven or nine years, the remains are sometimes disinterred and the bones are washed.[26]

In addition, there are elaborate wake and burial ceremonies. The wake can continue up to three days from nightfall to daybreak to protect the dead body from harmful accidents or influences such as the traversal over or under the body by certain animals, or from the possibility of the shadow of a living person falling on the body. (p. 290) The consequences are said to include another death in the family or the vampirization of the dead person. In order to keep everybody awake and watchful, a ceremony was added, in the past, to the wake, a rather gay one, with masks, costumes, skits and dancing. The masks represent "old people" generally, or devils or animal spirits. There are animated conversations, mockery and repartee between the principals and the community, reportedly to help people have a good time and forget death, to give courage in the face of death, or to remind the living that the dead have the same pleasures as the quick. (p. 296) To my mind, the general significance of the above is once again to celebrate the connection between the real world and the sacred realm of magic and the dead.

Burial customs last for the entire year in some villages, such as in Oltenia, and include the planting of a tree on the grave of the deceased and the singing of hymns at the grave by a selected group of villagers. The hymns urge the dead onward on their journey to the other side, and to forget their connections and relationships to this world.[27]

*   *   *

The largest group of legends of were-wolves in my collection, forty out of a total of ninety-four, recounted the attack by a husband on his wife as they are in the fields raking and stacking the hay: "clothing in teeth"; see Thompson motif number H 64,2, The husband, who is occasionally older than his wife—his second marriage—and wealthy, leaves for the woods to fetch some branches for steadying the stacks, or water, or to relieve himself. He returns as a wolf, dog, or pig, and after jumping up at his wife, tears her outer garment, but then departs. He returns in human form and scoffs at her tale of struggle with a ferocious animal; as he opens his mouth in mocking laughter she notices strands of her garment in his teeth. There are different endings for the tale. She either leaves him, divorces him, stays with him (after he acknowledges his problem), or drops dead. The story appears to teach us that older, wealthy men who seek a young second marriage partner are to be avoided; in the same way that a legend of an older man, also a were-wolf, who, after the death of his first wife of cancer, took a young woman in order "to have children by her." A large dog, which the informant said was the devil, appears in their loft one night and cannot be dislodged, and the attempts to wound it—to verify whether it is a were-animal—are fruitless. The young wife of the household gives birth some time later, and the infant is all covered with hair, gives off a disagreeable odor, and dies after a brief existence. Avoid older, wealthy prospective husbands, but also the first legend suggests that wives that are abused have the opportunity to leave their offensive mates and return to their parents' house or marry another.

The second largest group related the encounter of a hungry but weakened wolf in the woods that prowls back and forth near a camp fire. The forest workers throw the wolf some bread and pork fat and the animal departs. The wolf's benefactors are later welcomed, fed and hugely rewarded in their village destination by a man who confesses that he was that very were-wolf. Thus, even a potentially rapacious animal is to be shown compassion; with fortunate results for all.

Another rather large group, eight stories, dealt with the encounter of a pack of wolves lying in a circle around their human leader. The chance intruder departs unseen, or is allowed to depart because he referred to the wolves as "rams" or "sheep." In this way he conferred a normal aspect on the scene and preserved the secret nature of the relationship. Two other groups of five and six legends tell of efforts to stab a strange-looking dog or an invading wolf with the result that the were-animal immediately regains his human shape, or the human being is later identified by the wound which he bears but which he suffered as a were-animal. Two legends describe the were-wolf enchantment as a punishment due to the sin of the victim's parents who conceived the child on the eve of a high religious holiday, and a third tells of a male child born on Easter who becomes a were-wolf. There are twenty-two other legends in which a were-wolf is encountered, is said to roam with normal wolves, or in which an animal changes its animal shape before the eyes of the person who later related the story.

When the informants were asked the reason for the existence of were-wolves, eighteen of the thirty-two responses related the condition to the possession of a little tail, extending from the spinal column,[28] and which in eight of the responses was the result of allowing an already weaned infant to return to the breast. The next largest group, six, simply stated that the enchantment fell upon the victim at his birth; as a curse, a punishment,[29] or merely by chance. One person ascribed the ability to change one's shape to birth with the caul, that is, a part of the placenta adhering to the baby's head.[30] Three responses explained the condition as due to an illegitimate birth from parents who were themselves a second or third generation of illegitimate children.[31] The remaining four ascribed the condition to bad blood or evil spirits; two to the fact that the subject was the seventh of all male children, or had been born with fur down his front.

Thirteen people testified that a child conceived on the eve of Christmas, New Year's or Easter would be born with deformities, "animal characteristics," or be unlucky or malicious.[32]

In response to the question about their behavior, eight people out of thirty-three responses, answered that they come out on the eve of important religious holidays, to prowl and attack people. The next largest group, seven, replied simply that they attack people, and in particular, those with whom they have quarreled. Four others added that they attack cattle and sheep;[33] especially if they have quarrelled with the owners. Eight responses commented that they prowl at night; three said with other dogs, if they are were-dogs; three said that they were attacked by real dogs.[34] Four miscellaneous responses included "they prowl on the road"; "they change their shape when dogs are in heat"; "they can't rest until made to bleed"; and, "they are robbers and crooks."

Fourteen out of thirty-four statements concerning the mode of transformation said that they will immediately revert back to their human form if made to bleed.[35] One response stated that this terminated the magical spell. I have already discussed this item in relation to the etymology of the term *pricolici* in Romanian; namely, the idea of a reversed skin. Fifteen other responses cited somersaults, "three," "nine," or an unspecified number as the mode of change to and from a wolf or other were-animal.[36] The remaining two responses said simply that the transformation takes place "at night."

In the discussion of attitudes toward were-animals, five out of eleven responses replied that there is no persecution or scandal; one has to be cautious, but they are "allowed by God; a part of the world," and they are treated just like everyone else. Four informants insisted that there are no more *pricolici*. And of the last two, one said that the were-wolf is unaware that he changes his shape, and one stated that they are a species of *strigoi*.

The largest group of legends of witches, that is, seven of the twenty-three total narratives of this group, depicted them stealing milk from cows or sheep, or, if the animal had no more milk, then blood would flow in its place. Pavelescu asserted that this was the most common motif associated with witches in his collection of 1945.[37] The means used to cause the milk, or blood, to flow vary from merely walking through the village repeating "de aici o țîră, de aici o țîră" ("from here a little, from there a little"), sticking a knife in a tree near a flock of sheep, merely pointing it at the ceiling of one's house, or directly sucking from the cow in human form or as a cat or a dog. Two legends describe the disenchantment of cows that would give no more milk; one by a magical ceremony, and a second by recourse to the knowledge and skills of another witch in a neighboring village. In one legend, a victim of a witch of his village goes directly to the latter to request the witch end his suffering. The wretch had made a hasty obscene comment as he heard the incantation of a passing witch calling out the milk. The remark "by my ass you will" had caused the subject to bleed from the anus until the witch agreed to cure him, on condition that he cease his mockery of the witchcraft. In four stories of this total group, witches were identified as women who bathed in the river under a bridge in the middle of the night or in the dead of winter when there was a sheet of ice on the water. This group of narratives is probably related to the belief that witches cannot drown, no matter how deep the water; that they drown other people by riding them to the bottom of the river;[38] that they bind the rain and cause droughts;[39] or bring floods to particular fields by bathing nearby;[40] or that it rains for two weeks after one of their number dies.[41] There are four tales of encountering a witch on foot in a cemetery, or, on horseback, a woman who has the reputed ability to bring milk into her home by sticking a pitch fork into the rafters of her house. In this instance, the woman promises the protagonist of the tale that his property will forever be safe from storms and lightning in return for his silence. The second story tells of meeting a witch "on the road"; the third of seizing a woman bathing in the river at night; and the fourth, by capturing a rolling cart wheel, which, having been suspended from a spike on the wall, turns into a young woman.[42]

Four of my legends of *strigoi* recount the return of the dead to their village. A man killed by stabbing came back to look for his wife and family; some of his neighbors told him the surviving family had moved away, and he abandoned his search. One tale relates that a deceased father of four sons, who, in life had been a *strigoi pe lucru* ("wizard for working"), had to be disinterred and compelled to rest in peace by dint of a stake plunged through the heart. A third story describes the regression of a young woman from death who visits her former village suitor in the form of a wolf. The young man beats the wolf off with a stick, brutally injuring it. He is reproached for this by the young woman later in her human shape, for she could consequently no longer be a "complete woman." The striking features of these stories are first the nonchalance with which the encounter with the walking dead is related; in particular the implication that the walking corpses can be spoken to, and dealt with as if they were alive. And secondly, the reproach of the "dead" young woman that the bruises she suffered from her real-life suitor left her less a woman (i.e., unable to bear children) than other "living" women. A final account of a visit from the dead concerns the seventh of all male children who died by drowning and who, his mother believed, returned to haunt the family at night. The last tale of this general category of witches and vampires merely testifies to the existence of a man in the village who had been born with a tail and who became a wealthy property owner.

The forty-four responses given to explain the existence of *strigoi*-witches were heavily weighted (twenty-four) to the possession of a tail; of which one attributed it to "the Lord."[43] The remainder of this group of responses (twenty) were scattered over eleven versions of, at most, two or three incidences each. They included "weaned and let return to the breast," "they have fur down the back," "the third generation of illegitimate children," "born with the caul," "the seventh child or seventh female child," "unbaptized children who died," "their tail gives them the power to change into a wolf or a dog," and, for the dead *strigoi*-vampire, "a cat or other animal crossed over the body before burial."

A total of fifty-eight replies described the living *strigoi*'s behavior. The largest set in this group (twenty-six) stated they take the milk from cattle or sheep, and if the milk is depleted then blood must flow in its place; one respondent mentioned the use of a pitchfork stuck in the ceiling. Another significant set of responses (ten) affirmed that *strigoi* prowl on the eve of Saint Andrew's feast day.[44] The remaining answers (twenty-two) were distributed over nine statements, including "they take the power (*mana*) from wheat fields," "prowl at night, shrieking," "kill or otherwise harm people" (three), "don't do anything bad" (four), "change into a cat and suck the milk from cows," "come out of the grave and eat sheep and cattle," "don't assume an animal form," "fly on a broomstick and can disfigure people they meet," "the eve of Saint Andrew's is a carnival of the dead during which unbaptized children weep at their graves as do those who perpetrated evil in their lifetimes."

Concerning general attitudes toward witches, the largest number of comments, nine out of twenty-nine, contained the opinion that, although they are feared and precautions are necessary, as living members of the community, they are treated as other people; the expression that one "n'are să gindeşte despre ei," ("there's nothing to think about in their case"), sums up the feeling of their place in the common order of things. The next most prevalent attitude (eight responses), was that people do not make as much of them as before, or that these are "just stories," or, that one has not seen any *strigoi* for a long while and nobody really knows anything about them. Four people declared that there are diverse kinds of witches; those with special abilities for getting milk, making money, taming wolves, cooking, working, or drinking. The remaining eight responses were distributed among five statements such as "one doesn't reveal the witches' identity" (two), "people with a tail have a connection with the devil" (two), "*strigoi* have extraordinary strength and will power" (two), "*strigoi* cannot remain in the earth" (one), and, "every man has two natures, demonic and divine" (one).

Rubbing garlic on doors, windows and cattle on special days of the year was the main type of countermeasure recommended for witches and ghosts. Thirteen of the twenty-six total pronouncements expressed this belief; six advising it on Saint Andrew's eve, and one each for the eve of Saint George's and Saint John's (the summer solstice) feast days.[45] The next largest set of opinions, three each, advised consulting a neutral magician (*vrăjitor*), or driving a stake through the heart of a suspected walking dead person.[46] The final seven statements of one incidence each recommended amputating the tail,[47] making the sign of the cross when in danger, having a priest recite prayers to disenchant animals or people, bury the dead face down,[48] reverse the mirrors in the house of a deceased before interment, distribute garlic at the church at Easter and watch to see who doesn't eat his or her portion, or simply, that "disenchantment is possible."

In a related group of beliefs concerning wolves, thirty-nine in all, fourteen informants named a particular saint as the protector of that animal, and described their responsibility in the ordering of wolf behavior.[48] For example, of the total of twelve, five ascribed the loss of cattle and sheep to possible punishments for failure to abstain from meat on Saint Peter's day, one for refusing to obey the interdiction on weaving and sewing on Saint Andrew's eve.[50] In addition, wolves howl on Saint Peter's day for something to eat; Saint Andrew, on the eve of Saint Peter's feast day, gives his wild charges permission to eat certain animals.[51] Further, in accordance with Saint Peter's dictum, a wolf surprised at sunrise with his mouth closed cannot kill or eat any animals that day (four statements).

In an amazing symmetry with the *strigoi* beliefs, but with a decrease in dramatic intensity away from the human to the animal realm, six informants stated that the seventh (or ninth) wolf cub is not a wolf but a *lynx* that crawls through the vagina into the interior of a cow and devours its vital organs. And finally, there are the usual incidences of a single response that include putting garlic on the doors of farm buildings to protect the animals from wolves; using the ashes of pulverized wolf bones for skin disorders; catching a wolf and putting a spell on it to protect the sheep from all wolves; the belief that a wolf will kill as many sheep as it can (as many as seventy-five in the space of a few minutes), but will eat only one; and the attribution of a bitter, evil man's behavior to his "wolf fur." Lastly, two informants testified to the powers that are obtained by blowing through a wolf's gullet: to arrange a marriage, to cure a son of fearing, or to bring harm to personal enemies.[52]

There are some counter remedies against witches and vampires listed in earlier collections that I did not record during my fieldwork. There are, for example, the customs of breaking dishes, turning jars and pots over to prevent the vampire from using them to open the door,[53] or blowing the Alpine bugle horn (*buciumul*) to scatter away unwanted spirits.[54] Furthermore, Bîrlea lists the practice of stuffing stones, millet, beans, eglantine, garlic, rotten eggs or nails into the orifices of the corpse or in the coffin, or alternatively nine sprigs of sweet basil together with the body of the animal that may have passed over or under the deceased. (p. 383) Pavelescu's work, finally, adds the mixing of garlic, lovage, common celandine and sulphur in salt and feeding it to the cattle before every important religious holiday.[55]

Some of the earlier collected material of were-wolf and *strigoi* legends shows, in comparison to the items from my records, that the lore has indeed undergone some changes in the twentieth century; specifically toward moderation and, perhaps, a decline in overall quantity. Already in 1935 Agnes Murgoci remarked on the first element in this evolution: "While the word *strigoi* generally denotes a a reanimated corpse like the *vrykolaka* of Greece and Macedonia, . . . its significance has become less terrible. Witches in Roumania are often little more than wise old women, or *babas* who in their turn are only less common than leaves of grass; they also attempt good deeds as well as evil." (p. 349)

As an example of a more bizarre fantasy, Ovidiu Bîrlea, relying on B. P. Hașdeu's and Niculița-Voronca's studies of, respectively the late nineteenth century and 1903, includes in the activities of the *strigoi* casting the evil eye, and penetrating into the stomach to devour the heart and suck the blood; witches and vampires in addition, travel great distances riding on a scutcher, a broom or a barrel, and they meet at a cross-roads where they fight until they fill up with each other's blood, wherefore they are immediately healed and reconciled. The winner of the fight becomes the leader. (p. 383) Marcel Olinescu's study from 1945 adds the following: after making love with some-one, the female vampire sucks his blood and in the morning the man finds a red stitch mark, as if from a needle, on his body. There are, nevertheless, despite the similarity of this motif to Bram Stoker's *Dracula*, no "groupies" or squads of human vampires created by the bite of, and under the control of a single, undead commander, plot-ting to invade other nations and to conquer the world.

The effect of all the foregoing is, it seems to me, to ascribe the persistence of were-wolves and witches among the people to the remnants of the other world that accompany the new-born infant in-to the human community. The tail, caul, animal features, fur down the front or the back, as well as the failure to properly socialize the child during weaning signify that there has been a faulty harmoniza-tion of the magical and human realms. Secondly, the material asserts the rightful existence in nature and human society of the widest pos-sible spectrum of beings and events. The mythological beings (and here I include the saints of popular tradition), make certain demands of respect and reverence for their protégés, their feast days, or their powers. Thus, disruptions in the human community are caused by the failure to honor these demands, or by the chance emergence of the mythical might of the underworld. In this latter instance, the ulti-mate effect depends on the social context of their emanation; that is on the individuals who receive it.

If there are to be advantages in the communication between the three worlds of humanity, nature and the other world, if magical as-sistance can be obtained from the saints, the *rusalii, ursitoare* or *sân-toaderi* for the health, protection and well-being of the community, then, the folklore of Romania seems to say, one must expect that the forces that provide these advantages may not be handled or controlled without some risk to human society. The source of the power that makes someone a wizard with special talents may also provide him with the potential to harm his fellow villagers, or may oblige him to undergo certain transformations; that is, to assume the shape of an animal. In relation to legends of were-wolves and witches in other countries , Romanian tradition allows them to retain their status as members of the society, and shows, excluding the reanimated dead who have abandoned the human realm, that the disturbance can be managed without excommunication or banishment.

The folk beliefs, legends and ceremonies reaffirm the affinities between the separate worlds, and, at appropriate times and in appropriate ways, summon the forces of the non-human for the enhancement of village life. The function of Romanian folk mythology is, therefore, to mark clearly the limits of human society and to provide the means to identify and protect against unforeseen incursions from the animal and chthonic realism.

The practical effect of the above is, in sum, to preclude the necessity of vigilante groups or scapegoat specialists. The were-wolf and vampire are explained by the body of mythological stories and axioms. They constitute a "social" phenomena; the responsibility for which may be borne by a family, a generation or an entire community. The "vampires" of pathological case studies, the history of crime, or the pages of Gothic novels do not have a place in Romanian folklore. Rather, like the most famous representative of horror stories, Dracula, they seem to have come to the West.

CHAPTER SIX

ROMANIAN PARALLELS IN WORLD-WIDE FOLKLORE

The most striking feature of Romanian were-wolf and vampire legends is their strong similarity to the traditions of Slavic-language peoples, among whom the belief existed as early as the eleventh century. Wilhelm Hertz's well-used nineteenth-century study of the were-wolf attributed the very origin of the belief in the walking dead to the Slavs: "the specific Slavonian form of the universal belief in spectres," he contends, and continues, "certainly vampirism has always made those lands peculiarly its own which are or have been tenanted or greatly influenced by Slavonians."[1] Without totally subscribing to Hertz's views, one can say with assurance, I think, that in the Slavic-language areas, and those over whom Slavs have exerted an important influence, as for example the Romanians, Albanians, and Greeks, the legends of were-wolves and vampires is widespread, and their transmission is broadly supported by folk beliefs. My intention, in this chapter, is to trace the world-wide existence of beliefs and narratives that repeat and illuminate the strikingly complex and rich corpus of Romanian traditions. I am not searching for the original forms nor attempting to prove the claims to progeniture of one nation over another. Nor am I, in sum, presenting a case for the credibility of wolf-man or vampire legends, or an attempt to identify a causal physiological syndrome of a disease such as porphyria,[2] rather I seek to show that the disparate elements I have gathered from Romanian folk mythology are indeed related to lycanthropy and fear of the dead, and provide a balanced and sensible explanation for extraordinary phenomena.

It is in the Slavic tradition that the vampire has eclipsed the were-wolf after gaining exclusive use of its name: *vlkodlak*. The wolf-man has lost its role in life as, ironically, it was believed to become a vampire after death—a belief that is found in Romania, Greece, and East Prussia as well.[3] In Danzig, Germany, for example, legends recommend burning a deceased were-wolf, because it will otherwise find no final peace, awakening each day after interment in ravenous hunger, thence to consume its own hands and feet and then to emerge from the grave to kill cattle and suck the blood from sleeping people. The dead bodies of its victims are discovered the next day with a small wound on the left breast.[4] The East Prussian *blutsauger* ("blood-sucker") especially prized the blood of a young woman.

The original terms for were-wolf in Bulgaria (*vrkolak*), Serbia (*vukolak*), and Russia (*vlkodlak*)—Greek *vyrkolakas*—now exclusively designate a vampire.[5] The Romanian variant *vîrcolac* which is rarely used today seems also to have lost the human wolf motif, and is moreover rarely used for the walking dead either. In Greece, according to a classic study of Greek folklore by J. C. Lawson, during the tenth-century migrations into Greece, the Slavs brought with them their belief in were-wolves and vampires where they continue in a conceivably identical form today. The newly arrived *vrykolakas* supplanted the old and unused *lycanthropos* and replaced the native beliefs and terms for the undecayed dead that did not accurately express the notion of the raging predatory destruction of the Slavic vampire.[6] The vampire, as we commonly understand that term, is a Slavonic conception.

There is, in Roman Jakobson's opinion, a "common Slavic patrimony in demonology," and a "common Slavic were-wolf tradition" that found their first widespread cultural expression in the eleventh-century epic poem of the were-wolf Prince Vseslav of Polotsk.[7] The great-grandson of the famous Prince (Saint) Vladimir of Kiev, Vseslav was a dramatic figure, born with the caul, adroit, swift, incredibly lucky, whose exploits became, in popular accounts, fused with ancient Russian beliefs about were-wolves. The extraordinary astral phenomena that preceded and accompanied the prince's birth, added to his allegedly precocious behavior as an infant and adolescent, sufficed to create his myth. Eclipses of the sun and moon occurred in 1064, and were seconded by a "large red star with bloody rays."[8] When only an hour and a half old the infant prince is said to have roared out a demand for armor instead of swaddling clothes. At twelve years, he mastered the art of metamorphosis and at fifteen led his first hunting expedition.

The belief in the magic power of the caul is especially strong in Slavic countries, and in its simplest form is a token of good fortune.[9] Both forms exist in Romania, that is, as a sign of an auspicious future and of lycanthropy, and, in addition, in Norse-Icelandic mythology it bestowed the power of second sight and ability to change into animals.[10] The Slavic were-wolves in Serbia, Bulgaria, Slovenia and Czechoslovakia were also the causes of eclipses that signify the triumph of the nocturnal element. They devour the sun and the moon because they love darkness.[11]

The oldest recorded variants of the *Veslav Epos* date from the 1870's in western Siberia, and exhibit traits that are common to were-wolf and vampire legends alike.

> Volx, or 'magician,' the son of a princess and a serpent is born with a caul which he wears upon him at the insistence of magicians. His supernatural power and his eagerness to shed blood are predestined and make his mother and Mother Earth tremble. He grows up with miraculous speed, and the same wizardry speed marks all his deeds. Possessing the gift of second sight, he masters the art of magical transformation and leads the double life of a prince and a were-wolf. He is omnipresent, exceedingly crafty, and wonderworking; the huntsman's luck accompanies his predaceous, venturesome quest for power over the animal and human kingdoms. In vain his prospective victims strive to escape. Intimately allied with the forces of night, he threatens the sun itself. Where he comes running in wolf-shape, there the earth becomes stained with blood, and vampiric ghosts hover over his abode. Glory and suffering are inseparably intermingled in the course of his life as a werewolf—hunter and beast, persecutor and persecuted at the same time. (p. 352)

This legend gives us a better understanding of the underlying mythology of the wolf-man and vampire figures in the broader Slavic tradition, and of a rationale that goes beyond mere erotic blood lust. The hero, as representative of the forces of darkness, was a hunter and a warrior who threatened every living creature in his continuing quest for complete mastery over the animal and human kingdoms.

In the general Slavic popular traditions, birth with the feet foremost,[12] or with teeth, are signs of future were-wolves.[13] In addition to devouring the sun and the moon, the were-wolf may kill cattle, suck the milk from cows, mares and sheep, strangle horses and attack humans. (p. 229) The wolf-man may also, however, be the victim of an enchantment. In this case, he harms no one, and awaits the cessation of the spell. Were-wolves may change their shape at a particular season or time of the year; just as they may determine the moment of their metamorphosis themselves by donning a wolf's pelt.[14] In Serbo-Croatian, Slovene, and generally among the Slavs, there exists a protecting spirit to guard the household against the ravages of the were-wolf.[15] The *krsnik, kresnek* is described as a "sun-hero" who, at other times is pictured as a vampire or a lynx (*rîs*) who comes out

of the grave at night to drive away evil spirits, or is himself a representative of evil.[16] Parenthetically, the inclusion of the lynx recalls
the five folk beliefs from northeastern Romania, that define the seventh or ninth *wolf* cub as a lynx that devours the insides of cows.
Lastly, Saint George is sometimes called the patron of wolves, and
there is the tradition of the wolf leader who calls his charges together
once yearly and assigns them their prey.[17]

Some of the alternative terms that designate Slavic vampires are
upir, upior, ancestor of the English vampire, *wieszczy* and *montwiec*
from Poland, *oboroten* from Russia, *pijavica* or *vedomec* among the
Slovenians, *kruvnik* in Bulgaria and *lampir* from Bosnia; all joined to
the aforementioned *vlklodlak.*[18]

As in Romania, the circumstances that pre-destine people to lycanthropy return to mark them as future vampires. The Germanized
Slavs of East Prussia, as in Romania, hold the belief in vampires from
children two-times weaned, or who are born with the red stain of a
birth mark.[19] The presence of teeth at birth and a scum (caul) on
the head produce the Polish creatures known as *obyn* who, if the
teeth are not extracted, later turn into vampires and begin their ravages by devouring the flesh of their own bones.[20] Additional causes
of vampires in Schneeweis are Christians who convert to Islam, priests
who say mass in a state of mortal sin, or infants whose godparents
stumbled while reciting the Apostles' Creed at their baptism. (I, 8 &9)

A further detailed list of the conditions that create vampires occurs
in W. R. S. Ralston's two studies of Russian folktales and folksongs.
Wizards, witches and were-wolves, outcasts from the Church and its
rites, heretics and great sinners, apostates, suicides, victims of a parental curse; a dead body over which a cat or a young boy have vaulted,
a bird has flown, or the wind from the Steppe has blown will turn
into the walking dead.[21] Others born from the union of a witch and
a were-wolf or a devil, or those who drink themselves to death will
know the same fate. The Croatians call the vampire *pijawica* (from
the root *pit,* "to drink"); the Serbians, referring to a red-faced hard-
drinking man, assert that he is "blood-red as a vampire"; and both
the Serbians and Slovaks denote a hard drinker as a *vlkodlak.*[22] One
of my informants in the village of Şanţ (Bistriţa-Năsăud) called
heavy drinkers "strigoi."

A preliminary reading of this data suggests again that vampires
arise from exaggerated behavior, inordinate appetites, disrespect for
established ritual, and the disruption of the smooth transition from
the land of the living to that of the dead. The very same conditions

are described in Romania, except, with respect to my informants, the victims of a parental curse, the union between a witch and a were-wolf or devil, or the action of a young boy, bird or wind passing over the deceased's body.

According to several Slavic sources, a vampire whose teeth are like steel will use them to gnaw through all obstacles, then he will go forth to destroy first the babies in each house followed by the older inhabitants. Sometimes it is said that, as he feeds first on his own hands and feet, his relatives and then his neighbors sicken and die. After finishing his personal reserves of flesh, he ventures out to destroy cattle, to torment his relatives, to suck the blood of the next of kin, or to create a din in the attics of houses where he has entered by the keyhole or through the cracks. And the belief exists, lastly, that the slain victim of a vampire will himself become a vampire.[23]

The only certain methods of destroying the walking dead, in Slavic belief, is to drive an aspen stake through its heart with one blow, to chop off his head with a grave-digger's shovel, or to burn the body.[24] Of course there are countless variations in instruments and targets. Ashwood, hawthorne, maple, blackthorn, whitethorn stakes, as well as needles, sharp pieces of iron, spades or thorns may be driven into the head, heart, navel, or belly.[25] One may choose also to scorch the corpse with a hot iron. In Poland, pre-burial precautions number the use of coins to weight down the eyelids, tying the mouth closed, covering mirrors and stopping the clocks in the dead person's home, and keeping watch over the corpse until interment—a ceremony which, as in Romania, often became infused with merriment.[26] The Serbo-Croatians, furthermore, are known to paint a cross in tar upon the door or to place an axe before it.[27] These methods recall rubbing garlic in the form of a cross in Romanian traditions.

In Serbian, Slovenian, and Bulgarian lore, a vampire will rise up from the grave either for a period of forty days or after that amount of time has elapsed.[28] Alternatively, he may wait for the full moon, as in Poland, or merely a waxing moon.[29] When he issues from the grave, it may be from a hole in the top of the earth mound, or he may do so with his feet emerging first.[30] The vampire may be possessed by the Devil, in the same way that the Devil is said to blow up the skins of dead people.[31]

Schneeweis' study, finally, depicts the vampire's appearance as a pouch with no bones, filled with blood; with flames leaping from the mouth, blood-shot eyes, covered by shaggy hair, and, withal, gaunt and lean. (p. I, 9) Vakarelski recorded that they are similar to the shadow of a man or an animal (which recalls a legend I collected in Petroasa, Bihor, and published in 1977). He notes that vampires are afraid of fire, light, wolves (!), water and thorns. (p. 239) Machal includes the description of the appearance of souls of the dead as "jack-o'lanterns"; that is, "will-o'-the-wisps" which we will find later occurs also in Louisiana, in the United States. (p. 230)

The *călușari* ritual which I have included in my discussion of the mythological context for Romanian wolf-men and vampires has a Slavic counterpart in the *rusalye* festival which also took place at Pentecost. In this latter context, however, the connection to vampires is more explicit in that the *rusalye* is designed to secure the good will and favor of those who died a violent death. (p. 311) The Bulgarians in southern Macedonia, Machal concludes, moved the *rusalye* to Christmastide, and the chief characteristic of the festival became its warlike games (p. 312); that is, probably, the sword dance motifs that are essential elements of the common "hobby-horse" and *călușari* ceremonies in Romania and western Europe.

A final explanatory mythological element in Romania for werewolves, the goddesses of fate (*Ursitoare*) who preside over the birth of each child and assign its destiny, is present among the Slovenes of northern Yugoslavia. There, the *Sojenice* or *Rojenice* decide a child's fate and the time and manner of its death. The German *Norns* are mentioned as further representatives of the goddess type.[32]

Slavic villages, like Romanian communities, expend a great deal of energy and time for the feasts in memory of the dead; the *pomniki* is celebrated at short intervals after a death and again on its anniversary. Ralston attributes this to the survival of a faith in the continued residence of the dead in the place where they have been buried, and their capacity for physical suffering and certain pleasures of the body.[33] We find a similar concept in the Daco-Getan cult of Zalmoxis discussed above in Chapter Three. The term *pomniki* from *pomin* (remembrance, prayers for the dead) is close to the Romanian *pomana* (gifts or alms). And the underlying concept is identical, with nevertheless in this latter country, the effort to assist the deceased in his passage to the other world. The Romanian requiem mass at the end of forty days is said to mark the end of the dead person's temporary residence on earth, and his departure for the other world. Forty days is also a crucial number in the folklore of vampires of Greece to which I would like to turn now.

An interesting and revealing attempt to ascertain genetic affiliation and to separate native from borrowed vampire beliefs occurs in J.C.

Lawson's *Modern Greek Folklore and Ancient Greek Religion.* Lawson postulates three main sources: pre-Christian Greece, ecclesiastical
law, and Slavic lore. He lists the causes for the dead to emerge from
their graves and matches them with their probable origin. For example, the walking dead are said to come from those who do not receive
the full rites of religious interment; those who perish by a sudden or
violent means, including suicides, or, in the regions where the *vendetta*
is invoked, whose murders go unavenged. The children conceived or
born on one of the great festivals, such as Christmas, or between
Christmas and Epiphany, and children still-born are next. Then come
those who die under a curse, especially from a parent, or self-invoked,
as in the case of perjury. After this comes the class of the excommunicated, unbaptized or apostate; men of evil and immoral life in general,
or those having engaged in witchcraft in their lifetime. And finally,
vampires are created from those who have eaten the flesh of sheep
killed by a wolf, or those over whose dead body a cat or other animal
has passed.[34]

Using the frequent incidence and types of Greek curses that cast
the fate of non-dissolution and decay on the future dead body of the
object, such as "May the earth not receive you," or "May the ground
refuse to digest," as well as the native Greek terms for the undead,
and the ancient emphasis on the vendetta added to the milder types
of some legends in Greek tradition, Lawson arrived at an equation of
affiliation. That is to say, of the causes listed above, only three can
be said to derive from pre-Christian, pre-Slavic Greece: those who
die without full and due rites of burial, those who are the victim of a
sudden and violent death, or murdered, who remain unavenged, and
those who lived a gravely immoral or evil life. To the Slavs, Lawson
attributes the belief in revenants caused by eating the flesh of sheep
slain by wolves—a tradition which, in Greece, occurs only in the area
of heavy Slavic domination—and the belief in the vampirization of
the dead over whom animals have passed before their burial. (p. 407)

The rationale for Lawson's conclusions rests first on the unfearing
use of curses that condemn the transgressor to be a vampire. This
would hardly be the case, he reasons, if the subject fully understood
the horrible end he and indiscriminate numbers of others in the community faced at the hands of the object of his curse. Secondly, native
Greek terms for the undead are significantly less terrible and more
matter-of-factly descriptive. They are the equivalent of "drum-like"
(from the expanded and tight nature of the swollen flesh), "fleshy,"

"incorrupt," and "sits-up-in-the-casket." (p. 381) The fleshy homo-
logues in Bulgarian sources mentioned above suggest some cross-
fertilization here. These terms exist today only in the outlying islands
such as Cythnos, Cythera, Cyrprus, Crete and Rhodes which remained on the far side of the Slavic invasion. Thirdly, Lawson cites a few
legends in which the undead, although called a *vrykolakas*, or "vampire," are nonetheless harmless or even amiable individuals. For example, there is the story of the shoemaker of Santorini who continued
to frequent his house to mend his children's shoes, draw water at the
reservoir, and cut wood for the use of his family. Or the shoemaker
of Maina who resumed his work and continued to live with his wife,
the latter's pregnancy forced her to reveal the truth. There was, finally, the field-laborer of Samos who continued secretly to plow the
fields at night. (p. 395) These more humane vampires recall the Romanians' belief in the *strigoi* nature of those blessed with unusual
talent, and the legend of the *strigoi pe lucru* ("wizard for work")
who was forcibly fixed with a stake to prevent his seemingly harmless return to life to carry on his labors.

The Church, having inherited the belief in the incorruptibility of
dead bodies under certain conditions, in Lawson's view, made that
situation an article of faith, an instrument of fear, and a deterrent
from apostasy. The ancient Greek concern for burial and dissolution
into the earth created a more probabe feeling of pity for the people
who did not find integration therein, but instead returned from the
grave. This would explain the seriousness of the execration levied to
prevent someone from resting in peace. Sophocles' description of
Antigone's courageous burial of her outlaw brother Polyneice in de-
fiance of King Creon, and the resulting tragedy, is, moreover, a re-
minder of earlier attitudes toward death and dissolution. In a not-
able instance of violent destruction wrought on the living by the
avenger of tradition, Lawson underlines the focused and reasoned
nature of the retribution, in contrast to the unreasoning and indiscriminate fury vented by the *vrykolakas*. In the ancient world, the
avenger sought only his murderers, or at the most, those who had
failed to carry out the vengeance they owed the victim. (p. 458) The
examples of revenge that he recalls to us are, among others, the
tragedy of the House of Atreus.

The period required for the dissolution of the body is, according
to custom, forty days in popular lore, or three years, as fixed by the
Church. Forty days was, in times past, the limit of the period during
which the supply of food and other physical provisions was obligatory.

At present the gifts of food generally continue until the third anniversary when exhumation takes place (p 540) In Romania, the period before exhumation is five to seven years. On Crete, furthermore, after forty days, all hope of natural decay is past, and the dead man becomes a "confirmed" vampire. (p. 488)

The most common method of destroying a revenant in Greece is by burning the body, in contrast to the use of the aspen stake in Slavic tradition. Today, the power of the priest's prayers is sufficient to metaphorically "burn" the suspected walking dead man. And a final method of protection is to fire a shot from a revolver into the casket.[35] The vampire belief is virtually non-existent in the folklore of western Europe, except in cases of were-wolf legends that describe the onset of metamorphosis after death. Nevertheless, in the state of Massachusetts, the Greek *vrykolakas* has found its way to America, where immigrants from Arcadia and Adramiti (near Smyrna, Asia Minor) maintained the traditions. Their vampires are quite often confused, nevertheless, with the seductive water fairies, the *neraides*.[36] On the other side of the continent, in northern California, logging communities repeat the belief that garlic will protect one from vampires—belief and remedy have possibly remained there after the Russian migrations and settlements north of San Francisco.

In southern Illinois and in Mississippi, tales of witchcraft are nearly identical with the *strigoi* witch and vampire motifs of Romanian and Slavic cultures. The "Egypt" area of Illinois produces legends of witches in the form of pigs and hares that steal the milk from cows and leave them weak and sick. The panic countermeasure is to draw a picture of the suspected felon, fix it to a tree and fire silver bullets into it. In the particular legend, the witch was immediately wounded and promised to leave the community if the bullet were extracted from the tree.[38] The "Bold Witch" of Tennessee and Mississippi is a corporeal ghost that likewise sucks the cow dry of milk.[39]

Louisiana maintains the French folk belief in the will-o'-the-wisp; in particular, as the soul of a dead person ordered to return to earth to do penance for his life's sins, but instead plays nasty tricks on people. The Louisiana *fifollet* from the French *feu-follet*, may also be a vampire seeking the blood of a child, or lastly, the soul of a child who died before he was baptized.[40] Let us recall here the Slavic identification of the "jack-o'lantern/"will-o'-the-wisp" as the soul of the dead people who lead the living astray and "strangle them."[41] The Norman French designate the "phosphorescent light" that dances over certain graves as the mark of a damned soul which will shortly emerge as a were-wolf.[42]

Sorcerers and vampires are closely identified, furthermore, in Haiti and the Bahamas. The Haitian zombi is a dead body that has been resurrected by a witch and used as its slave or robot.[43] The Bahaman "hag" slips out of her skin to suck the blood of babies and sleeping adults.[44]

As we make our way eastward across Europe to Asia, we find that German children born at the new moon are destined to become witches and vampires. Moreover, suspected German vampires are disinterred and coins are set in their mouths to prevent them from further "biting" and sucking blood.[45] The special time for Albanian witches, called *shtriga* (see the Latin *striga, strix*, and the Romanian *strigoi*) are especially powerful during the first week in March. And the Albanian precaution against vampires is to burn or hamstring the corpse.[46] The Chinese have vampire legends, and one of them is repeated in Dudley Wright's *Vampires and Vampirism* of a wife falsely accused of murdering her husband. The true criminal was a vampire whom the authorities discover in its grave with the slain man's head tucked under its arm. The arm is cut off, and fresh blood gushes forth; the victim's head had previously been drained.[47]

The Philippine Islands furnish us with a mythological figure that rivals the Romanian folk traditions in its complexity and breadth of distribution. The "Aswang" appears at times as a vampire, a viscera sucker, a man-eating were-dog, a vindictive witch, and a carrion-eating ghoul. As a beautiful maiden who sucks the blood of her husband, it uses the pointed tip of a mosquito-like proboscis to pierce the jugular vein. As in Romania, the were-dog is considered the victim of an undeserved affliction that is more appropriately a cause for sympathy.[48]

The lore of were-wolves is unusally strong in Germany, France, French Canada, the state of Pennsylvania, and Haiti. The tradition also exists in Italy, Sicily, and more rarely, in Spain, Portugal, and their South American colonies. It is interesting to note that the were-wolf to vampire after death progression is reversed in western Europe. In France, for example, the belief existed that evil men would become wolf-men after their death. The Normans recounted in legend that King John Lackland of England, for instance, was condemned to wander as a lycanthrope after his death in 1216: "he could not retain the peaceful possession of his grave."[49] Furthermore, at the beginning of the nineteenth century, Norman priests used to inspect cemeteries at night to check on the behavior of the inhabitants, and if they perceived that one of the dead that was damned to the infernal regions showed signs of becoming a human wolf, they opened the grave, and, with a brand-new shovel, cut off the head of the cadaver and threw it into the river.[50]

The designation "werewolf" is at least as old as circa 1000 in Germany; Burkhard von Worms defined the term used by the common people as "a man who can change into a wolf, when and how he desired."[51] Gervaise of Tilbury, writing in about the year 1210, attested that the were-wolf transformation at the period of changes in the moon was not uncommon.[52] The wolf metamorphosis in the twelfth and thirteenth centuries were less directly attributable to the Devil than they were to become after the papal bulls against witch-craft and heresy in the late fifteenth century. The twelfth-century *Roman de Guillaume de Palerme et de la Belle Melior*, carried its own lengthy subtitle: "was the son of the King of Cecille, and by fate and incredible adventure became a cowherd. And finally he became the Emperor of Rome under the guidance of a were-wolf, the son of the King of Spain." The *Lai de Bisclavret*, a late twelfth-century romance by Marie de France, based on Breton lore, restricted itself to retelling the treachery of the were-wolf's wife who stole his clothes during his metamorphosis, thereby preventing him from regaining his human form. Nothing is said of the cause or origin of the condition.

By the end of the fifteenth century, however, the situation had radically changed. The overriding impulsion became the pact with the Devil, by means of which the future were-wolf gained the ointment or liquid with which he effected the transformation. Jean Bodin's late sixteenth-entury French treatise, *Le Fléau des sorciers*, describes the process by which confessed witches changed back and forth from men to wolves, and, while in the wolf state, admitted murdering young children. The fundamental concept of this brand of were-wolf, as distinguished from the subjects of Romanian legends, is the notion of blasphemy and revolt against God, together with the contract with the Devil. Included in the French variants is the punishment of nightly transformation into a wolf for seven years as a penance for blasphemy and metaphysical rebellion. In Normandy, the penitent might regain his human shape if his blood were made to flow from a wound between the eyes or from a wound inflicted by three cuts of a knife.[53] The seven-year length of the curse and metamorphosis is common in many areas of France in the north, west and south.[54] During this time, the penitent must travel through seven counties per night;[55] he is given the locations of secret chapels where he may hear mass—as a part of his expiation[56]—and if he dies in the course of the seven years, his soul is the eternal property of the Devil. (p. 165)

Other types of reluctant were-wolves in France are the prey of the Devil in revenge for unpaid services he has rendered to them, or those people who have in some way incurred the demon's wrath. (p. 160) Still others unwittingly find themselves covered by a wolf pelt that the Devil had thrown over them, or try on a belt that the Devil had left behind. (p. 161) Anyone who touches a wolf skin that was temporarily or unknowingly left behind by a were-wolf whose soul was "damned" risks becoming a were-wolf himself. (p. 164) A modern version of Bodin's testimony is found in Upper Brittany in the legend of the wolf "leader" who achieved his transformation by means of a liquid in a bottle that the Devil had given him.[57] The use of a magic liquid for animal transformation is also spoken of in Brittany, but in one particular legend it was part of a vampire story in which several families lose their flocks of sheep to an unknown animal small enough to pass through a narrow hole to suck the blood of the sheep.[58] In Sicily, the sight of a wayside shrine and a crucifix or a madonna will throw the lycanthrope to the ground full of fear and trembling.[59]

In the Middle Ages it was generally believed, according to Montague Summers, that any man denounced from the pulpit and who refused to reconcile himself with the priest and confess the crimes for which he had been denounced, became a were-wolf. (p. 222) Paul Sébillot explains the malediction in Normandy and Poitou as a reference to a witness of a crime who is unwilling to testify against the guilty person. The witness is then liable to become a were-wolf.[60] In Lower Brittany anyone who abstained from confession or holy water for a period of ten years would be struck with this same animal metamorphosis. (p. 55) Such a curse could also be inherited from one's parents. (I, 285) Excommunication from the Church was another sufficient basis for the lycanthropic spell both in Brittany and southern Languedoc, and, in continuing similarity to vampire beliefs in Greece, criminals who had escaped justice suffered the same fate.[61] This latter is, further-more, an interesting modern repetition of the ancient etymology of *warg*, "wolf" and "outlaw."

The immediate reversion to human form by the were-wolf whose blood has been made to flow from a wound which is very common in Romanian lore is likewise very common in France, Germany, Sicily, Canada, Pennsylvania, Spain, and South America. In Normandy, as I have mentioned, one speaks of three cuts of a knife between the eyes. To cause the blood to flow brings immediate reversion to the human form,[62] and, at times, an end to the punishment.[63] The same belief in the cure by drawing blood is found in Sicily;[64] the Canadian and

Pennsylvanian lore derives from French sources.[65] The exception that proves the rule exists in France where it is also believed that loss of blood by the human wolf prolongs the punishment for another seven years.[67]

The legends of human leaders of wolf packs in Romania find an echo in France, mainly in the western and central regions, where the intruder is allowed to depart in the company of two wolves to his home where he is instructed to feed the wolves under pain of death.[68] A vindictive wolf leader directs his charges against the neighbors with whom he has quarrelled. At other times, a refusal to extend hospitality to him or to feed his wolves will bring rapid decimation of an offending villager's herds, or revenge on a particular farmer and his family.[69] Motifs identical to these occur in my collection from Romania.

The belief in a were-wolf's destiny for children conceived or born on Christmas which we discussed in relation to Romania and Greece is, moreover, also found in Mexico, Italy and Sicily. In Sicily and Italy the tradition affirms that birth on Christmas eve compels one to periodic transformation to a wolf during the week of Christmas and New Year's Day.[70] Notwithstanding the "irreverence" of a birth at this time of the year, or the violation of ecclesiastical canons as in Romania, the *periodicity* of the obligation to change into a wolf at Christmas Tide, during Advent, and on Saint John's day which was common belief in the Middle Ages,[71] is related, I believe, to the mythological legacy of pre-Christian festivals of the winter solstice and the late-winter lupercalia and anthesteria festivals that were designed to honor the dead and make use of animal spirits to revitalize the community. This was discussed in Chapter Two, but I repeat the concept here again because I believe that the idea of the periodic nature of animal transformation derives from the repetition of the cycles of nature; that is to say, winter and the notion of death, darkness and animal spirits, and spring fertilization and rebirth. Related also are the cycles of the moon, and in particular, the significance of its absence from the sky. For example, in Italian and Sicilian traditions, the child conceived at the full moon or the new moon will become a were-wolf; as will he who sleeps outdoors on a given Tuesday (or Wednesday) or Friday in summer with the light of the full moon shining on his face.[72] In England, the metamorphosis is likewise related to the changes of the moon..The Slavic were-wolf and Romanian *vîrcolac* are said to devour the moon and the sun; that is to say, to cause their disappearance from the sky. And Claude Gaignebet's study of the traditions of the pre-lenten carnival underscores the significance of the new moon, that is, the absence of the orb from the sky on February first, to the end of winter and the inauguration of the celebration. The point I wish to make here is that relating the conception or birth of a child to a particular time of the year—winter—with its accompanying cycles of the moon, a season that historically has been the period of honoring the dead and masquerading as animals, when the sky was at its darkest, is very likely responsible for the notion of the recurrence and periodicity of the transformation to a were-wolf. Lycanthropes seem to be allied with nocturnal powers, death and winter, but the festivals that included these elements combined with them the healthy theme of fertilization and community renewal; that is, the symbolism of the approaching spring.

Besides the were-wolves we encounter in Europe, America and Asia, there are, in Africa and other parts of the world, animal transformations that result in hyaenas, leopards, lions, and tigers. The Berbers of Morocco repeat stories of men who can change themselves into hyaenas at nightfall and resume their human shape in the morning. The well-known story of the Budas of what was called Abyssinia in what is now Ethiopia were a tribe of iron-workers and potters who were thought to be able to change into hyaenas.[73] The belief in the ability of certain men to become lions and leopards and afterward to kill their enemies is discussed by several visitors in Africa.[74] The collection of Chinese legends by a Jesuit missionary, Leon Wieger, contains several stories of lycanthropes, including one which traces a wounded wolf to a peasant's hut where an identical cut reveals the human wolf's identity. (p. 154) In Japan there is a group of were-fox superstitions. (p. 155) A source of early Celtic history recounted the legends of witches who changed into hares to suck the cattle for their milk, with versions from Wales, Ireland and Scotland.[75] Among the Magyars of eastern Europe, witches assumed the form of horses and cats. The story is told of an errant horse that was caught and shod. The next morning its human form is found with iron shoes on his hands and feet. (p. 208) MacCulloch relates here that Burchard of Worms spoke of certain *Parcae* who at birth inflicted a fate on the newborn child to make him change himself into a wolf in later life. (p. 208) The *Parcae* were the Roman goddesses of destiny, the "fates" that we have discussed earlier in Chapter Three as the Romanian *Ursitoare*. Some form of the belief in were-wolves is found in the Netherlands, India, Indonesia and Cambodia.[76]

The Spanish word for were-wolf, *lobombre*, testifies to the existence of the creature in popular lore, but, although not unknown, it occurs very seldom in popular traditions.[77] The *lobis-homen* of southern Portugal is believed to be a secretive and mild creature that turns into a wolf at a crossroads by turning around in circles rapidly before falling to the ground groveling and howling. (p. 167) The were-wolf curse that falls on the seventh of all-male or all-female children is also known in Galicia and Portugal.[78]

As I have listed the elements of the belief statement regarding the transformation to a wolf, in this chapter, along with the means to recover the human form, it became increasingly clear that parts of the mythology of were-wolves are dramatically widespread throughout the world. It is equally impressive, however, that Romania has in its folk traditions an outstandingly coherent and well-integrated corpus of belief and legend that incorporates most of the themes identified in cultures from Russia to Africa and India to Indonesia. It is obvious that there has been a great deal of diffusion from the Slavic peoples to the Balkan states, and fieldwork in western and south Slav villages might reveal a comparable degree of cohesion and integration of the traditions. But until the opportunity is found to verify that hypothesis, and a recent book announces the disappearance of the vampire beliefs among European Slavs,[79] Romania remains a country of truly rich and pulsating folk traditions that maintain the stability of village life and protect its members from vigilante groups and inquisitorial witch hunts.

APPENDIX A

LEGENDS OF WERE-BEINGS

I. Were-wolf husband attacks wife; is recognized by threads from her clothing in his teeth. (See Thompson motif number D 113.1.1; II 64.1; Reidar Christiansen, *Migratory Legends*, FFC No. 175, p. 58.)

1. Şanţ (Bistriţa-Năsăud), August 1, 1977.

"A man and his wife were working in the hay. The time came for his transformation. He was a *tricolici* and she didn't know it. He told her to climb up on the stack and to stamp down the hay. Then he went off to the woods. An animal came out— a pig. It jumped up at here; she defended herself with a pitch-fork and wounded it. The pig went off and the man came back. He was bleeding from a face wound. She said, 'A pig tried to eat me.' When she climbed down she saw part of her skirt in his teeth. They divorced and no more was said of the *tricolici*."

2. Lesu (Bistriţa-Năsăud), July 30, 1977.

"A man and woman were stacking the hay. She was on top of the pile using a pitchfork.

The man went off to the forest and in his place there came a big dog. It leapt at her, made the sound of 'hap hap hap hap,' and ripped her blue over-skirt.

The dog left and the man came back. She saw bits of blue threads in his teeth."

3. Şanţ (Bistriţa-Năsăud), July 28, 1977.

"A husband and wife went to work the hay stacks. He was a *tricolici*. Her husband left while she was up on the hay stack. A pig came at her and leaped up and tried to bite her. She de-fended herself with her red shawl. —No, it was a dog; pigs can't jump up.

The dog left and the husband came back. She told him what happened and he laughed; then she saw old red threads in his teeth.

They separated."

4. Şanţ (Bistriţa-Năsăud), July 28, 1977.

"A man and woman. She said, 'It's going to rain.' He says, 'Don't worry, let's go work in the hay.' (He felt his time of transformation was coming over him and wanted to be in nature.) He told her to get up on the stack and stamp down the hay. Then he said,—'I've got to go off for a short time, but don't be afraid of what you might see.'

A dog came. It jumped up and wanted to bite her, but couldn't reach her. She beat it with her shawl, which was red, until it was torn to shreds. The dog left.

The husband came back and she said, 'Where were you? A dog tried to kill me.'

He said, 'Oh, it was probably one of the dogs guarding the sheep. Anyway it could't reach you.' And he laughed. She saw bits of red thread in his teeth. He was the *tricolici*.

They separated. He remained alone because people knew he was a *tricolici*."

5. Şanţ (Bistriţa-Năsăud), July 27, 1977.

"A man and woman were working the hay, making a hay stack. She was dressed in red.

He told her to stay in the clearing while he went off to the woods to get some tree branches for poles for the stacks. He left and a little while later a dog came and attacked her. She defended herself with a pitchfork, wounding the dog in the face, but not before the dog had ripped her skirt. The dog left and after a time the man came back. She said, 'Where were you? A dog tried to kill me. . . . Hey, what's that wound on your face?' He said he'd had an accident in the woods and laughed. When he laughed, she saw bits of clothing in his teeth.

She left him."

6. Josenii-Bîrgăului (Bistriţa-Năsăud), August 3, 1977.

"A man and woman go off to stack the hay. The man leaves and a dog comes and attacks the woman. She defends herself with a pitchfork. She wounds the dog and makes it bleed. The dog leaves and the man comes back."

7. Sibiel (Sibiu), June 17, 1977.

"Some young people from the village were out in the fields somewhere one day. One of them said, 'If a big dog comes along , don't be afraid; he won't hurt you.'

Then a young man left. And a dog came along. It attacked one of the girls and tore her clothes. The dog ran off and the young man returned. The girl saw bits of her clothing in his teeth. She knew he was the *pricolici*."

8. Gura Rîului (Sibiu), June 20, 1977.

"A wealthy man had married a poor woman. He was a *pricolici*, but she didn't know it. One day they went out to cut and stack the hay. She was on top of the pile and he threw it up to her. Then he said he had to go to the woods to relieve himself, and he left. All of a sudden, a big dog came and jumped up at her. She took the pitchfork and defended herself. She had on a red skirt and the dog ripped it off. She didn't wound the dog, but it left. Her husband returned. She said, 'Where were you? A dog tried to kill me.' He said, 'What's that over there?' and looked away. She saw bits of her red skirt in his teeth. She said, 'What's the matter with you? You're the *pricolici*!' They went home. She told the neighbors that she wouldn't stay with him. She left for Bucharest—where the chief of the devils lives. She took a job as a housemaid in the home of the Prime Minister, Bratienilor. The man remained in the villages, and, after a while, died. The woman never returned."

9. Rășinari (Sibiu), June 20, 1977.

"A woman was attacked by a big dog when her husband had left for a short while. She fought the dog off.
When the man came back she saw bits of her clothing in his teeth."

"The *pricolici* is no more a man; it is totally a dog. But the other dogs attack it."

10. Tilișca (Sibiu), June 21, 1977.

"A rich (elderly) man married a poor woman younger than he to have children. He was a *pricolici*, but she didn't know it. They were going along in the forest. He said, 'Wait, I have to relieve myself.' He left, and shortly after a huge dog came and attacked her. It ripped off her clothes, but she defended herself and drove it off.
The husband came back and she said, 'Where were you? A big dog tried to kill me!'
As he looked away she saw bits of her clothing in his teeth. She said, 'You were that dog! You're a *pricolici*.'

11. Holod (Bihor), August 5, 1977.

"A woman went with her husband to make hay stacks. They made a stack, then the man said he had to go off somewhere. He came back as a wolf and attacked her. She defended herself, but the wolf ripped her clothing. The wolf left.
The man returned. His wife asked him where he had been and

told him she had been attacked by a wolf. He laughed and as he did she saw pieces of her clothing in his teeth.

She left him and married someone else. No more is known of him."

12. Hidişelu-de-Sus (Bihor), August 5, 1977.

"My father told me: A man and woman were working the hay. The woman got up on top of the stack. After they finished one the man said he wanted to go off for a little while to sleep. He turned into a wolf and came back. He attacked his wife. She defended herself by offering it her skirt. The wolf left and the man came back. His wife said she'd been attacked by a wolf. Then she noticed he had bits of her skirt in his teeth. This happened in a place called Tasad a long time ago. The man's name was Ion Florea."

13. Suiug (Bihor), August 7, 1977.

"A man and his wife went out to work the hay. After lunch he left to get some tools. He became a wolf, and returned and attacked the woman, standing on the hay stack.

She shouted and cried. There were some men in the neighborhood, and the wolf left. The man returned in its place. She said that she had been attacked by a wolf. He said, 'How so, I've not heard or seen anything.' He talked on and she saw bits of clothing in his teeth.

They went back home. And on the way, he changed into a wolf again. She shouted and fled. She left him. Nothing more is known of the wolf. This happened somewhere near here."

14. Suiug (Bihor), August 7, 1977.

"A man and wife were living in the village. He was a *strigoi*, but she didn't know it, until one day when they went off to harvest and stack the hay. While they were there, he left and a wolf came back in his place. The wolf attacked the woman and ripped her skirt, but left. The man came back, and his wife told him what had happened. 'It ruined my skirt.' He laughed and she saw pieces of her skirt in his teeth. She knew he was the *strigoi*. But he said, 'Don't worry, I only become a wolf at certain times.' They stayed together."

15. Coneui (Cluj), Cluj Archives, No. 2000 Ii, 1971.

"A woman had married a *pricolici*. One day he left the house and said, 'Don't be afraid of what comes back.' A dog came up into the house. It attacked the woman and tried to bite her, chasing her around the house. She succeeded in tying it up to one of the ceiling beams. The dog had ripped her clothes and some threads remained in its teeth. The dog got loose and ran off. Soon the man came back. The wife told him what had happened and then realized he was the *pricolici*. She left him and got married to someone else."

16. Şeredei (Sălaj), Cluj Archives, No. 2283 Ie, 1975.
    "A man and his wife went to the field to work the hay. The man went off and a wolf came. The wolf ripped the woman's skirt and left. The husband returned; the wife saw bits of her clothing in his teeth. She realized that he was the *pricolici*. She left him."
    "A *pricolici* can be a cat or a dog."

17. Pria (Sălaj), Cluj Archives, No. 2274 Iaa, 1975.
    "A man went off to make hay with his wife. While they were haying, he went off to the woods.
    A wolf came out and attacked the woman. The wolf ripped her skirt, and then, after a time, ran off. In a little while, the man came out of the woods. The woman asked him where he was all that time, because she had shouted for him when the wolf attacked her.
    He laughed and she saw bits of clothing in his teeth."

18. Pria (Sălaj(, Cluj Archives No. 2270 y, 1975.
    "A woman went off to work the hay. The husband went off to his job and said he would come back after a while. Where the woman was working, a dog came and ripped her skirt. The dog left. When the husband came, she told him what had happened and asked where he was when she needed him. 'A dog tried to eat me.' The husband laughed, and she saw bits of her clothing in his teeth.
    They told other people in the village who also laughed."

19. Pria (Sălaj), Cluj Archives No. 2270 Ie, 1975.
    "A husband and wife go out to make hay. Both are working. She climbed up on top of the stack. He threw the hay up to her. At a given moment, he is obliged to go off to the woods. He changes into a wolf. He returns and tries to rip off her skirt. At a given moment the wolf leaves and the husband returns. The woman tells him what happened and asks, 'Where were you? A wolf tried to eat me!'
    The husband begins to laugh and she sees bits of clothing in his teeth. She dies."

20. Pria (Sălaj), Cluj Archives No. 2265 Ir, 1975.

"A man went to the fields with his wife to make hay. She got up on top. Then he went off.

A wolf came and dug at the hay stack until the woman fell down; then he attacked her, ripping off her clothes. She called for her husband. The wolf ran off.

After a time the husband came back. 'Where were you?: she asked him. 'I was looking for the handle of a rake.' She asked him why he had pieces of clothing in his teeth. He admitted he was the wolf and said when the time came he had to do it."

21. Şeredei (Sălaj), Cluj Archives No. 2283 Iy, 1975.

"There was a wife, a young woman, who went off with her husband to hay. The husband went off to the forest and the wife stayed at the hay stack.

A wolf came out of the woods and ripped her dress. The husband came back 'dressed as a man'; as he was when he had left. The wife asked him to lie down with his head on her lap. She saw bits of her clothing in his teeth and realized he was the wolf. The wife left him."

"I heard this from my father."

22. Cizer (Sălaj), Cluj Archives No. 2287 IIa, 1975.

"There was a couple. The woman climbed up on the hay stack and the man gave her the hay. The man said, 'Wait, I've got to go to the woods.'

After fifteen minutes, she saw a wolf coming towards her. The wolf came and kissed her. She became very frightened and began to moan and cry, thinking the wolf would eat her. Then she began to shout for her busband; 'Pavele, a wolf is eating me.' The husband didn't come. The woman fell unconscious. After a while, the wolf went away and the husband returned, and found his wife lying there. He asked her, 'Maria, what happened?'

'*Vai de mine* ("woe is me"), a wolf came and tried to eat me.' The husband picked her up in his arms and took her home. He told her not to be afraid and began to laugh. The woman saw pieces of her clothing in his teeth. She left him."

23. Cizer (Sălaj), Cluj Archives No. 2288 Ig, 1975.

"A man with his wife went to the fields to hay. After the work, the husband said, 'I'll go to the woods and cut off a branch to put on top of the stack to protect it from the wind.'

He went to the woods and became a wolf. He came back to his

wife but didn't hurt her except to tear her clothes; then he
went off. The husband came back with a piece of wood in his
hand for the stack. The wife told him a wolf had torn her
clothes. The man replied something and the wife saw pieces of
her clothing in his teeth. She recognized him [as the were-wolf]
but didn't say anything, and they went home. The woman told
others in the village what had happened and she separated from
her husband. At night the husband came to her house in the
form of various animals."

24. Pria (Sălaj), Cluj Archives No. 2263 IIu, 1975.

"A young man who was a *strigoi* married a woman from another
village. One day they went to harvest and stack the hay. She
climbed up on top of the stack. He went off and when he came
back he was a wolf and jumped up at her.

He ripped her skirt. The woman yelled for her husband to come
and help her. The wolf left, and a neighbor came to help her
(his name was Paricanești).

When the husband returned the wife told him she had shouted
for him because a wolf had attacked her."

He laughed and she saw bits of clothing in his teeth."

25. Drighiu (Sălaj), Cluj Archives No. 012118, 1972.

"A man got married, and when his time came to change into a
wolf, he went off with his wife to make hay.

He left her suddenly without saying why. And a wolf came back
in his place. She defended herself with a pitchfork. Finally, the
wolf tore her clothing. She was very frightened, but the wolf
left.

The husband returned. 'Where were you,' she asked, 'a wolf
attacked me.'

He laughed and she saw bits of clothing in his teeth. She was
so afraid she died."

26. Cărăsău (Bihor), Cluj Archives No. 2285, Ic, 1975.

"A man went with his wife to do the haying. When his 'time'
came, the man went off to some place. I don't know, perhaps
he turned a somersault.

A wolf came back. The woman was very frightened and yelled
'Where are you, man!' She defended herself with a pitchfork,
but the wolf still jumped at her and ripped her skirt.

After a time, the man realized he shouldn't be doing what he
was doing because she would recognize him. He left. He returned
as a man.

The wife complained, 'You left me and here's what happened. A wolf tried to kill me and ripped my dress to pieces.' The man began to laugh. The wife cried, 'You! You were the *pricolici*. I see a part of my dress in your teeth.

She left him. People are born, pre-destined to be *strigoi/pricolici* and when the time comes they have to become them."

27. Vîntere (Bihor), Bucharest Archives, 1972.

"A woman went with her husband to the mill to grind wheat. They passed by a forest and he changed into a wolf. The woman shouted for help; she didn't know who it was.

Her husband reappeared. As they went home she told him what had happened. He laughed and she saw bits of her clothing in his teeth. She realized that he was the wolf. They divorced."

"This happened two years ago in Vîntere."

28. Roşia (Bihor), Bucharest Archives, 1974.

"A woman married a *strigoi de lup* who was gone every night. The next morning she asked him where he'd been, but he wouldn't speak about it, for fear she'd leave him if she knew.

One summer they had a serious argument and then went off to work the hay. Two wolves came to where she was working and ripped off her red skirt. They left.

Her husband came back and she asked him where he'd been, saying that two wolves had tried to kill her.

He laughed and she saw bits of her skirt in his teeth. She knew he was a were-wolf."

"I heard this from an old man who tended the cows fifteen years ago."

29. Topa-de-Sus (Bihor), Bucharest Archives, 1974.

"Two young people got married. She didn't know he was a *strigoi de lup*. He ran with the wolves and ate sheep. They were in the forest. The man stopped to drink in the stream and disappeared. A wolf came and attacked the woman. After a while the husband returned and she saw bits of her clothing in his teeth."

"Such things exist. How do they get along? People give them something to eat, so that they won't do harm to the animals. People see someone entering and leaving the forest; they know he's a *strigoi de lup*. If you see him in the forest you give him something to eat. Once after someone had quarreled with a person known to be a *strigoi de lup*, he lost a sheep."

30. Roșia (Sibiu), Bucharest Archives, 1971.;
"A man was gone for nine years from his house. He was with
the were-wolves (*pricolicii*). They turn somersaults and become,
once again, men.
A woman made a haystack. The husband went off for poles,
and changed into a dog and came back. She took her red belt
in his teeth. She realized he was the dog. She died and he remained a *pricolici*. He was gone for three years with the *pricolicii*, and when he returned, he was an old man: 72 or 73 years
old. He lived for a few years in the village. His name was Todoran
Bătrînul. He had heavy eye-brows; could scarcely see through
them, and was a powerful man. Everyone knew, but nobody
said anything. He was a good man. Today, he'd be shot."

31. Bîrgăului-Bistrița (B-Năsăud), Bucharest Archives, 1973.
"The couple was working the hay. The wife was on top of the
stack; the husband throwing up the hay. As they worked, he
asked her if something came would she be afraid?
'Why? What?'
'A dog, wolf, pig.'
The husband disappeared. She remained with a pitchfork ready,
watching both sides. A dog was approaching fast; it jumped up
on the stack. She didn't panic, but wounded it in the face. It
bled, and disappeared.
She stayed there. Her husband came back, bleeding. They
divorced right away."

32. Șanț (B-Năsăud), Bucharest Archives, 1956.
"A couple is working the hay; the wife on top of the stack, the
husband throwing up the hay. As they are working, he asks her
if she would be afraid of something that came at her.
'Why? What?'
'A dog, wolf, pig.'
The husband disappeared. She remained with the pitchfork
ready, watching. A dog came running, fast; it jumped up on
the stack. She stabbed it with the pitchfork, and it ran away.
Her husband came back, bleeding. He denied that he was the
dog, until they matched his blood with that on the pitchfork.
They divorced."
"*Pricolici* are dogs and wolves, but certainly dogs. They run in
the shadows of houses and buildings; they don't run on the
open streets. During the Christmas, New Year's and Easter holidays you can hear them going 'ooom, ooom,' and everyone
knows the *pricolici* are out."

II. Feeding a hungry wolf brings reward:

  1. Holod (Bihor), August 5, 1977.

"A man with three children was working in the forest making wooden pots. He sent the children home to bring back the cart and oxen and he stayed in the forest. He made a fire for a meal, and began to fry pork fat.

A wolf came to the fire, staying on the other side timidly and tamely. The wolf lifted a paw and showed it. It had something in it; a thorn or a piece of wood.

The man removed it and gave the wolf some bread to eat. The wolf left.

The children returned with the oxen; they loaded the pots and departed. They went to a nearby village, but nobody bought their pots. Then they stopped at a house for lodging. An old man in the house with a bandage on his hand invited them in. He told his wife to prepare them a meal. The old man had come out when his servant announced their presence at the gate.

The host then showed the pot-maker his hand and told him that he, the host, was the wolf who had come to his fire for assistance. He added he had been also cured of his were-wolf spell by that act of kindness and because the pot-maker had given him some bread. The host told him to leave all his wares there and take anything he wanted: corn, flour, anything."

  2. Pria (Sălaj), Cluj Archives No. 2270 Z, 1975.

"A man went off to make hay on the edge of the village, and made a fire to cook pork fat. A dog came. The man ate and the dog ate too, and then left.

After three or four years, the man went to Simlen to the market. He entered some place to eat. He saw a man with three glasses of plum brandy in front of him who called the new man over to eat with him. Although the latter had never seen this host before they shook hands and he asked this stranger where he was from.

'From over there.'

After eating and drinking a glass of brandy, the man explained that he was the dog that was so hungry, and it was fortunate that the first man had fed him; otherwise he would have eaten him and taken all his goods."

  3. Şeredei (Sălaj), Cluj Archives No. 2283 Ig, 1975.

"A hunter was in the forest, and at meal time he made a fire to cook some pork fat. A wolf came up to the fire. The man threw it some pork fat and bread. Some years later, the hunter met a man in a village who invited him to a restaurant and recalled to him the story of the wolf in the forest.

If the hunter had tried to shoot him, the wolf would have eaten him. But, since he hadn't, the man bought him a meal and gave him something to drink."

4. Pria (Sălaj), Cluj Archives No. 2265 Ip, 1975.

"There were three harvesters eating lunch and a wolf came out of the forest. One of the harvesters was named Nicolae Cristea. The men gave the wolf some bread and pork fat. The wolf ate and didn't come back.

After four years, Nicolae Cristea went to Marghita and asked a man where he could buy some wheat. The man said he'd give Nicolae three sacks.

'How much do I owe you?'

'Nothing, because some years ago you gave me something to eat when I was a wolf'"

5. Pria (Sălaj), Cluj Archives No. 2270 f, 1975.

"A man who was a shepherd up on the mountain was cooking some pork fat. As the meat was cooking, a wolf came and stood watching all the while.

The shepherd broke off a bit of the pork and threw it to the wolf. The wolf ate it and left. The shepherd went down to Marghita one day with his horse and cart to buy food.

He met a man who asked him where he was going. 'To buy some food.' The man took the shepherd home with him. He filled the cart with food, for no money. He explained that he had been the wolf; he was famished and hadn't even found a rabbit to eat. He explained that if the shepherd hadn't given him some bread and pork, he would have eaten him."

6. Şeredie (Sălaj), Cluj Archives No. 2283 It, 1975.

"A man from Pria was a *strigoi* on the mountain in Coasa. One night was clear with a moon.

Another man was on the mountain. He sat down under a pear tree and made a fire to cook some pork fat. A wolf came along and sat down looking at the man. The man didn't know what to do, but picked up a bit of bread with pork fat and threw it to the wolf. It ate and left.

That winter, the man went to Carei Mare with a cart filled with brooms to sell. A gentleman came out of the fields and said, 'Hey, I know you from Morleaca,' and asked him if he remembered giving him some bread and pork.

The man realized it was about the wolf. The gentleman invited
him to his house to eat.

The gentleman asked him to help him break the curse, but the
man said he couldn't and left."

"It's terrible to be cursed like that, but one can do nothing.
One must see it through."

7. Cizer (Sălaj), Cluj Archives No. 2288 IH, 1975.

"A man went off to the fields to hay. At lunch time, he made
a fire and put some pork fat on it to fry.

After a time, a wolf came to join in the meal. He threw the
wolf something to eat, and it went off. After some years, when
there was a shortage of food, especially bread, the man went
to Marghita to the mill to grind corn. He met the man who had
been the wolf; the man transformed himself 'when the time
came.'

The *strigoi* said he knew the first man.

'From where?'

'At one time I was very hungry, and you gave me some bread
to eat.

And he gave the first man a large sack of flour. He told him,
'One month I am a man and the next I am a *strigoi*; I was pre-
destined to it by the *ursitoare*.

III. The leader of wolves:

  1. Holod (Bihor), August 5, 1977.

    "In the town of Vîntere, there was a man who commanded the
    wolves.

    He was a *strigoi de lup*.

    He was treated just like anyone else, even though they knew
    what he was."

    "Both men and women can be a *strigoi de lup*."

  2. Hidișelu-de-Sus (Bihor), August 5, 1977.

    "An old man in a nearby town was a *strigoi de lup* and com-
    manded fifty to a hundred wolves. He simply turned three
    somersaults, turned into a wolf and the whole pack came to him.
    They didn't hurt anyone; only those with whom he had quar-
    reled."

  3. Vîrciorog (Bihor), August 6, 1977.

    "There was a wild man who commanded the wolves but didn't
    change into one."

4. Pestid (Bihor), Cluj Archives No. 2290 IIg, 1975.

"My father went into the woods near Reghin, with a sack of tobacco.

He went along for a while, then lay down and put his head on some hay.

A woman dressed in white appeared before him and told him to get out of there fast. He did. As he did he heard the sounds of a wolf wedding in the woods—*dînd, dînd, dînd*. He climbed up a tree but left the sack down below.

The wolves came and took the sack and threw it from one to the other.

The following day, he stayed up in the tree. That night he climbed down, picked up his sack of tobacco, and went home."

5. Pria (Sălaj), Cluj Archives No. 2265 Idd, 1975.

"Nenea Paru, an elderly woman, said two men went to Ciuciu, and up there they were walking to a field where they saw a woman spinning.

Next to her were many wolves.

'Good morning, where are you going with the 'sheep?' they asked her.

The woman said, 'It's a good thing you said 'sheep.' If you had said 'wolves,' you'd have been eaten. Don't say anything about what you've seen.'

The men returned hom and recounted what they had seen. A week later one of them died. Two weeks later the other one died."

6. Pria (Sălaj), Cluj Archives No. 2271 Icc, 1975.

"In Parîu Cornitului between Curiz and Pria, an old man told me about a young man from Curiz who went to a young girl's house in Boian each evening.

One time he saw a man surrounded by wolves. He wondered what to do, but it was too late. If he fled, the wolves would catch him, and if he went forward, the same thing would happen. He decided to go on. He bade them good evening and asked the man where he was going with those 'rams.'

The man said, 'You were blessed by God because you said 'rams,' otherwise you'd have been eaten. You can go on, don't be afraid from now on.'

He went on to his girl's house. On the way he stopped and hid to see what would happen. He saw the man giving orders to the wolves; to go in all directions and eat everything they found, but not to hurt the people. After giving the orders, he turned three somersaults and left.

Then he never went back by that route because he was afraid.
Now we don't know where their meeting place is."
7. Vîrciorog (Bihor), Bucharest Archives, 1972.
"I saw the Master, the leader of the wolves. I was with some
hunters in the forest. The wolf leader controlled the wolves
and wouldn't let them eat the hunters."
8. Vîrciorog (Bihor), Bucharest Archives, 1972.
"My father had an oven made of plaster. He went there one day
and there was a woman surrounded by a pack of wolves. She asked him where he came from. He replied, 'None of your business.'
She told him to take a particular route and not to be afraid,
but not to tell anyone what he'd seen.
He passed on, and had just about reached his destination when
he heard the wolves howling. My father was terribly afraid. He
thought they were going to eat him. She was truly a *strigoi de
lup*."
"Those born on Easter Sunday are obliged to be a wolf for
seven years."

IV. Identify the were-pig by the wound:
  1. Stupca (Neamṭ), May 24, 1977.
     "When I was young, I heard that Alexandru Căileanu changed
     into a pig and attacked someone who defended himself with a
     pitchfork.
     The next morning Alexandru was seen with a wound in the
     cheek."
  2. Șanṭ (Năsăud), July 27, 1977.
     "A pig was attacking and biting people in the village. Some night
     watchmen came along and beat it with sticks and wounded it
     with a pitchfork in the face.
     The next day they saw a man from the village with a wound in
     his face. He was a *tricolici*.
     When a *tricolici* dies, it begins to rain and doesn't stop until
     you dig up the grave, and turn him over, face side down."
  3. Șanṭ (Năsăud), July 27, 1977.
     "There was a man who could turn himself into a pig or a horse
     and who would roam through the village. Whenever he met
     someone in the village there was a huge battle. One time he
     was hurt; wounded in the face and immediately turned back
     into a man. He went right home to put something on his cheek
     and hide the wound, so that no one would know he was a *tri-
     colici*. He was ashamed of it.

He had received this curse because after he had been weaned, he was allowed to return to the breast.

But nobody believes in *tricolicii* any more."

4. Şanţ (Năsăud), July 27, 1977.

"Some people from Bucovina came to Şanţ. My father lived in the village at the time. One night as he was returning home he was attacked by a pig. He defended himself with a pitchfork, and wounded it in the face. The *tricolici* fled. His wife saw one of the Bucovina women the next day with a wound in her face. She was the *tricolici*, and they discovered later that she had a little tail at the bottom of her spine."

5. Lesu (Năsăud), July 30, 1977.

"My father saw a woman going on the road at night. She was the wife of the church cantor and she was a *tricolici*. He was attacked by an animal; he defended himself and wounded it with a pitchfork. Two days later the wife of the cantor came complaining about wounds in her back—in the exact same place he had hit the animal."

V. Make the were-being bleed and it will regain human form: (D 712.6)

1. Răşinari (Sibiu), June 20, 1977.

"*Pricolicii* (were-dogs) will kill other dogs and if made to bleed they will re-assume human shape. They have their power only at night, until 12:00. Otherwise they are men like any other."

2. Suiug (Bihor), August 7, 1977.

"A man changed into a wolf and sucked milk from the cows. The villagers wounded it with a pitchfork and it died, but before dying it turned a somersault and regained its human form."

3. Gîrbou (Sălaj), Cluj Archives No 1870 IIf, 1969.

"A were-dog came after the sheep. The dog slept for two nights near a shepherd, and then suddenly began to bite him. The shepherd called to his mates to come with sticks to beat off the dog. They wounded it and it began to cry like a man, as it ran off."

"At night a *strigoi* turns into a wheel and rolls through the village. One time a man caught the errant wheel, took it to his house and put an axle in it. Two days later he found a man with the axle through his mouth and sticking out his back [out the anus].

The man asked for pardon and asked him to let him go, saying he wouldn't come back. He let him go."

4. Gîrbou (Sălaj), Cluj Archives No. 07742/1, 1969.
"People saw a dog with the cattle, and when it was wounded, it began to speak like a man."
"We don't hear any more about them. When people don't have other distractions they talk about them."

5. Corneiu (Cluj), Cluj Archives No. 2000 Ii, 1971.
"Someone in the village saw a were-dog standing in the courtyard of a house. A boy ran after it and wounded it with a wooden staff. The dog ran off and a man came back and lay down on a hay stack. The next night he came back and the third night too."
"In general, if one wounds a *pricolici* and the blood flows, it becomes a man. Until its blood flows in a wound it must stay a dog. But it will turn into a dog again."

VI. Conceived on the eve of a religious holiday, born on Easter, is destined to become a were-wolf:

1. Pria (Sălaj), Cluj Archives No. 2270 g, 1975.
"There was a woman who had a son. Each evening the youth left. She thought he was going to a party in the village (in Cizer), but he would go to a tree stump. There he would undress, turn three somersaults and turn into a wolf. His father went there to watch. He waited for the youth. He saw a wolf come, turn three somersaults, and become his son and go home. He followed the boy home and went in. He told his son he knew what the boy did each evening.
The youth asked how he knew. The father said he'd been at the stump and had seen him.
The youth said, 'Too bad. I would have eaten you because you conceived me on a high holiday.'" [and caused this situation.]

2. Vîrciorog (Bihor), Bucharest Archives, 1972.
"A man had a child who would learn nothing. He tried everything to make him learn.
One day the boy was gone to the forest. The father followed. He saw the boy turn three somersaults and change into a wolf. That evening, the father said nothing.
At twelve years of age, the boy got lost in the forest. The parents quarreled. 'Was it because they had struck him that he became a wolf?'
That evening he came back. The next day he left, and the father followed. The boy changed into a wolf. The father fled home,

and said nothing. He related it to his wife, and said he was afraid
the son would eat them. 'What can we do?' 'Let him be, let him
be, he'd only get other wolves to eat us.'

Seven years passed. The son was no longer a were-wolf. The
father told him that he knew his secret, and asked him what he
had done. The boy said he'd have killed his father if he'd known
his father was nearby when he became a wolf. He had met a
young girl and had taught her how to become a were-wolf."
[And that's what broke the spell.]

  3. Bucharest Archives, Manuscript No. 4752, p. 18-19, from E. N.
Voronca.

"A woman and a man had two sons, one conceived on the eve
of Saint Nicholas' day, and the other on Easter eve. They went
through the forest, but the parents thought they were courting
young girls. But hiding behind a tree, their father saw them going to a place where there was a fire, and, rolling over and over,
they became wolves.

The two wolves strangled a man and a woman returning from a
wedding on horseback. A man bringing a letter from the mayor
saved himself from the wolves by making the sign of the cross
over and over until after midnight. The wolves became men
again, rolling over and over.

Before they returned home, their father got there and told his
wife to prepare to leave because their sons were were-wolves
and he and his wife would be killed by them.

Two days later, the sons saw the parents preparing to leave.
They asked them why? The father answered, 'Because you are
were-wolves.' The sons offered to leave, themselves. They said,
'What can we do? God sent this because you conceived us both
on high holidays.' The sons left."

VII. Encountering a were-wolf or shape-shifter:

  1. Tilişca (Sibiu), June 16, 1977.

"Some men came through the village late at night and saw the
Devil sitting on the gate of a house. They knocked on the door
and asked for something to eat.

The woman of the house climbed up into the attic to get something for them to eat. In the attic she saw a large black dog.
She tried to chase it out, but couldn't; she tried to wound it
with a pitchfork and make it bleed, but couldn't.

The man of the house was successful and wealthy. His first wife had died of cancer and he remarried with this woman who was thirty years younger in order to have children.

Some time later, the wife gave birth to a son. The *ursitoare* came the night of his birth. Three days after the birth, the windows and doors all blew open and slammed shut. Nobody knows how or why.

At nine months, the son became covered with animal fur; he stunk like an animal, and died.

The Devil was in that house."

2. Şanţ (B-Năsăud), July 28, 1977.

"My brother saw a big dog behind the houses, among the farm buildings. I saw a ram; the dog had become a ram. I saw a doll in front of the house. The ram had become a doll. This was the Thursday before Easter. It was probably a neighbor, since *tricolici* come out before high holidays."

3. Şanţ (Năsăud), July 28, 1977.

"A man was going through the forest, and came upon a *tricolici* that was first a pig, then a horse, then a wildcat, then a dog. It went alongside him.

He made the sign of the cross with his tongue, and it disappeared."

4. Şanţ (B-Năsăud), July 28, 1977.

"My father was going home New Year's Eve once when he felt something was following him. He began to run and the thing ran too. He ran directly into his house (there were no fences or gates). He looked out a window and saw a large pig. It stood on its hind legs and peered through the cracks in the door."

5. Holod (Bihor), August 5, 1977.

"One evening my uncle, 74 years old, was returning from Vîntere to Holod, walking on the railroad tracks. He came upon two horses that reared up and tried to trample him. They reared up again and changed into one man. My uncle raised his stick and got a closer look at the man. He had horses' feet. The *strigoi* fled."

6. Pria (Sălaj), Cluj Archives No. 2265 Io, 1975.

"My great-grandfather related that he was going up the mountain to Ciuciu with a cart of wood. It was winter. There was a lot of snow. He left the cart there and came back with the horses.

On the way back a wolf came out on the path. A voice called out 'Ion Indrioane, come back.'

The wolf began to howl and the man couldn't bear the voice. The wolf went off.

A month later, the man went to Oradea to sell fruit. On the way back he stopped at a small restaurant. Someone asked him, 'What are you doing with the wolf?' He said, 'What can I do?' It was a *strigoi de lup*; he would have been eaten."

7. Cizer (Sălaj), Cluj Archives No. 012133/1, 1973.

"A dog that came to my father's house, a long time ago, broke off some grape vines, but didn't eat them; only left them on the ground. My father tried to wound it with a pitchfork, but failed."

"They are born that way. I haven't seen it."

8. Pestid (Bihor), Cluj Archives No. 2286 Iz-IIa, 1975.

"Tatul Lazariki from Urvis said that wolves eat the sheep of the inhabitants there. There was a man who was going to the *stîna* [mountain shepherd's hut] , looking for something to eat. If he didn't get anything wolves would come and eat the sheep there. One evening I was going to the train station in Soimi and I met a man. The man asked me, 'Do you have a son in Baia? It's good luck you gave me something to eat.' (In general she made a lot to eat and gave it to anybody who came.) I noticed that he had a big stain on the back of his neck as big as a hand. After I got home, I went to the well for water, near the woods. I saw the man passing through the woods. He said, 'It's good you came.' The evil continued that night; more sheep were killed."

"*Pricolici*" turn into a wolf by turning somersaults."

9. Pestid (Bihor), Cluj Archives No. 2290 IId, 1975.

"My husband was a metal worker in Urvis. He knew a youth, an orphan. His mother was afraid of wolves and always went with her children. One night while on the road, she met a man. The man asked her where she was going; he said he knew she had a child and that he took care of him because she had given him something to eat.

The man left. The woman watched him and saw he had a big stain on the back of his neck. In the daytime, the man went out from the village looking for food. If the people didn't give him anything, he ate their sheep. She went with her child behind the village in winter; in all seasons she feared wolves, but never had any trouble.

She went home with her boy. Immediately she saw the man she had met on the road who had asked for food. She immediately brought him some. That night a neighbor lost ten sheep."

10. Altina (Sibiu), Cluj Archives No. 2278 IIn, 1975.
"In the village there was a man who took care of the cattle. He took the cattle off to the fields.
A wolf came. The man beat him very well. After a while a man came and asked him about the beating. The guardian said that he had beat a wolf, not a man."

11. Şanţ (B-Năsăud), Bucharest Archives, 1956.
"A woman was fetching a mid-wife in a village. She was being chased by a pig. Then the pig tried to bite her foot, and wouldn't let her pass.
She said, 'Go away, go away, *pricolici*.'
She freed herself and ran away."
"We know some people can change into animals. We know that. It was perhaps a *strigoaica*."

VIII. They run with wolves:
1. Poclusa (Bihor), Cluj Archives No. 08954/2, 1971.
"When a man changes into a wolf other wolves come and they go off and attack prey. After three days the were-wolf comes back very tired [*slab*]. He can transform himself at will. One time one of them left his wife behind for two or three years."
"Protection: garlic and the leaves of the fag [*mesteacă*]."

2. Hodişel (Bihor), Cluj Archives No. 2020 IIc, 1971.
"*Pricolici* roam with wolves and mate with cats. They are born with bad spirits. *Strigoi* are also born with bad spirits."

IX. Miscellaneous:
1. Săvineşti-de-Sus (Neamţ), May 22, 1977.
"The child born with a tail has the power to change into a dog or wolf. My father knew somebody who had this power."

2. Tilişca (Sibiu), June 21, 1977.
"I was with the sheep. All at once I saw a big shape, a shadow. The dogs barked, and lunged at it. It went away; chased away. It was a *pricolici* perhaps."

3. Tilişca (Sibiu), June 21, 1977.
"One day a woman from the village told me that she had gone to the market with a cart to sell four pigs in Sebeş. She had hired a gypsy to drive the horses for her. As night fell on the way, the gypsy ran off. She yelled, 'Where are you going?' at him, but he didn't answer.

Then she heard a great ruckus of snarling and growling of dogs. When he came back, he was all bloody and disheveled. They went on to the market. She related the incident to people there and they said he was a *pricolici*."

"*Pricolici* are just part of the world. Some people are musicians, or dancers; some are *pricolici*."

4. Sibiel (Sibiu), June 17, 1977.

"A man came from Rășinari to Sibiel. Everybody knew he was a *pricolici* [were-dog] because he had snakes in a pot in his house. He didn't fear them. He had a whistle to call them, and he had been seen at the edge of the forest whistling, and snakes came out to him. Perhaps he had the Devil in him. We knew he was a *pricolici* also because he rolled down a steep hill turning somersaults while dogs barked at him. One night I saw a big black dog in our courtyard breathing very hard, very tired and looking at me fixedly as if it were human. My husband said it was that *pricolici* from the village. He tried to wound it; to make it bleed, and make it turn back into a man.

The *pricolici* transformed himself every night until the cock-crow. The people didn't do anything to him by day because the man was unaware of his other existence. The people were frightened of him also, but it was something permitted by God. One day the *pricolici* put a mouse in a woman's pot of milk to make her give it to him. He was a robber and he duped people."

5. Șanț (B-Năsăud), July 27, 1977.

"A young man was returning from twelve years in the army. He still had his rifle. He entered a village. There was a light on in a house. He went in. There was no one except for a dead man lying on the table.

The young man climbed up in the loft with his rifle beside him. At 11:00 the door flew open and a big dog came in, and attacked the dead man. The latter rose up and fought the dog until 12:00 when the dog left and the dead man lay back down. The young man had his rifle ready all the time, but wasn't threatened.

The next day he went over to the town hall and asked why they didn't keep watch over their dead. The mayor said they did, normally, but this man was evil, and nobody wanted to keep watch. It was the Devil's job."

6. Forosig (Bihor), August 5, 1977.

"A man named Petre Leon brought a woman back from Bicaz to Forosig. She was a *strigoaica de lup*, but he didn't know it.

She undressed, turned three somersaults, and became a wolf,
They said she had a tail. There was no scandal, no fuss. The village doesn't do anything so that it doesn't react against them
like a wild animal. Their blood is not normal; it's wild."

7. Vîrciorog (Bihor), August 6, 1979.
"In my village they speak of a man who went out into the
fields at night. The next day some sheep were sometimes missing. They could see pieces of sheep's wool in his teeth. He had
a little tail at the end of his spine."

8. Cărăsău (Bihor), Cluj Archives No. 2021 IIk, 1971.
"A gypsy in wolf form ate a sheep and went off with it. He
took it up to the mountain. I don't know how long he stays a
wolf."
"The caul is a sign of *strigoi*."

9. Gîrbou (Sălaj), Cluj Archives No. 010542, 1969.
"*Pricolici*; they exist. I heard them when I was with the sheep
on Saint George's Day. They were in the air, fighting and making screetching sounds like a cat. Afterward I saw the broken
lances."
"The Lord allows this to go on."

10. Vîrciorog (Bihor), Bucharest Archives, 1972.
"I saw a man change into a wolf. I knew who it was because I
recognized his eyes and eyebrows."

11. Pestid (Bihor), Cluj Archives No. 2290 IIf, 1975.
"*Strigoi* can change into a wolf or a dog. They suck the milk
from cows or kill sheep. They look for food in the village. If
they don't get any, they eat the sheep. They turn three somersaults. They are born, predestined to it.
Strigoi suck the blood from children who die. Women know
how to use magic against them. *Strigoi* have the caul at birth;
if the mid-wife breaks it, the curse is prevented. The *strigoi pe
lucru* is very hard working, only that."

APPENDIX B

LEGENDS OF WOLVES

I. Saint Peter, Creator of the wolf:
1. Bucharest, June 25, 1977.
"Saint Peter wanted to create a being himself. He created the wolf, and became the patron and commander of wolves."

II. Saint Peter uses wolves to punish people who violate his feast day:
1. Tilişca (Sibiu), June 16, 1977.
"One must not eat meat on Saint Peter's day. Or else Saint Peter's wolves will punish the violator.
Some young girls ate meat during Saint Peter's day. They stored their provisions in the loft of a neighbor's house, where they could see anyone coming or going.
That night they went to bed in the loft of their barn. There was a big storm. They heard nothing and saw no one. But the next day, their bacon and pork had disappeared: Saint Peter's 'pets' had eaten them."

III. Wolves attack sheep; their ferocity:
1. Tilişca (Sibiu), June 16, 1977.
"One night my father said that if I want to go to the *hora* [village dance], I must bring in enough hay for the animals. I was going to the fields when I passed a neighbor's house with a high fence where wolves normally couldn't get in. All at once a wolf jumped over the fence, and killed seventy-five sheep in a flash. I had never seen such a thing in my life. The sheep that survived couldn't eat for three days. If I hadn't been there, the wolf would have slaughtered them all."
2. Răşinari (Sibiu), June 20, 1977.
"Wolves come into the town. Even a bear came in once and got a donkey for itself. My father had eighty-seven sheep killed by a single wolf. The wolves will kill all the sheep, but eat only one. One time seven wolves came toward a herd of sheep, and drew away all but one of the dogs. From another direction, more

[101]

wolves drove the sheep away. The lone dog fought with the wolves, but couldn't drive them off. The wolves killed almost all the sheep. If another dog had been able to help, they would have beaten the wolves."

IV. Saint Peter forces the wolf to keep its mouth shut:
1. Rășinari (Sibiu), June 20, 1977.
"Saint Peter does not always allow the wolves to have their prey. In the mountain two wolves came out of the forest for the sheep. The wolves were as big as donkeys, but they couldn't eat the sheep. Their mouths were closed and they couldn't open them."

V. Wolf and human birth:
1. Marginea (Bihor), August 8, 1977.
"A young woman gave birth to a baby with the head of a wolf. It was because of medicine she had taken."
2. Suiug (Bihor), August 7, 1977.
"A wolf and a woman have children. She went with it to its lair in the ground. After a time she decided to return home. She was followed to where she lived, and the children were killed."

VI. Giving food to wolves on the eve of Saint Andrew's Feast Day:
1. Barbana (Argeș), June 9, 1977.
"On the eve of Saint Andrew's Feast Day, a friend of my father's went into the woods where there was a meeting of the wolves. He brought a clay pot [oala] with him and yelled or howled through it. The wolves came to him and he gave them smoked meat as alms to tame them; to soften them, and make them less fierce toward man."

APPENDIX C

LEGENDS OF WITCHES AND VAMPIRES

I. Witches take the milk from cows and sheep; D 655.2; E 251.3.2.

1. Tilişca (Sibiu), June 19, 1977.

"My grandfather used to cut and transport wood from up on the mountain with his hired men. One day while in the forest they saw a flock of sheep. One of the companions asked, 'Do you want some milk?' The others thought he was joking, but he walked up to a tree, and stuck his knife into it.

Drops of blood began to run down it. The sheep had already been milked and had no more; therefore blood came. The sheep began to die because the spell continued on into the next day. The man had put the spell on them."

2. Tilişca (Sibiu), June 19, 1977.

"One day some men who work with wood, carving it, came through the village to sell their goods, and in passing looked intently at the sheep. From that moment on the sheep gave no more milk."

[*Note*: wood carvers are usually gypsies in Romania.]

3. Tilişca (Sibiu), June 19, 1977.

"There was a man who could make milk drip down from his attic merely by pointing a knife upward toward the attic. He was a *strigoi* who charmed the animals and stole their milk."

4. Tilişca (Sibiu), June 16, 1977.

"There are people who can get milk from sheep, even if the sheep are far away on the other side of the mountain, if they want to. If there is milk, they get it. If not, then blood. *Strigoi* take the milk from cows. They kill whoever sees them."

5. Tilişca (Sibiu), June 16, 1977.

"A man supposed to be a *strigoi* passed by all the doors of the village saying, 'De aici o tîră, de aici o țîră'; [a little from here, a little from there].

While passing by a household courtyard, where a man was relieving himself in the toilet, the man in the toilet said: 'Si din

curul meu'; [my ass you will] . The *strigoi* said 'fine' and went
on. The man began to bleed from his anus and bled for six
weeks.

Finally he remembered the words he had said to the witch. He
went to the witch and asked him to help him. The witch cured
him on condition that he say no more about it, and that he
never again be caught saying 'by my ass.'

6. Marginea (Bihor), August 8, 1977.

"There was a *strigoaica* [witch, female gender] in the village
named Mama Gabrieli. Once the cows gave no milk for two
weeks. She would change into a cat and go suck the cows' milk."

7. Vîrciorog (Bihor), August 6, 1977.

"Here in Vîrciorog, a long time ago, a woman was a *strigoaica*
and took milk from the cattle. She sucked the milk. She had a
coada [a little tail] . One day she was attacked and wounded
by a pitchfork, and that was how we knew she was the witch.
People were afraid."

II. Encountering a witch:

1. Tilişca (Sibiu), June 16, 1977.

"One time my grandmother met a female witch on the road.
The witch told her that if she said nothing, she would be all
right, but if she divulged her identity she would lose her head.
The grandmother was so afraid at night that she wouldn't walk
home from the train station (at Salişte) alone. When the witch
died, people said they saw her coming out of the river."

"*Strigoi* have a little tail, and in general, they sit at the edge of
town when the cows pass by. They chant 'de aici puţin, de aici
puţin,' [from this one a little, from that one a little] , and they
get the milk from cows."

2. Tilişca (Sibiu), June 21, 1977.

"My father told me that when he was young he heard that an
old man had gone into the cemetery and had lain down with
his head on a gravestone. He saw a woman on a horse passing
by the cemetery. He had a horse and followed after her. She
said, 'Don't say anything about this and your property will be
forever safe from damage from storms and lightning.' The
mother of this woman was a witch; my father knew her. She
could put a pitchfork into the rafters of her house and milk
would drip from it."

3. Şanţ (B-Năsăud), July 27, 1977.

"My father, when he was young and strong and didn't drink, and some friends were stealing pears from a neighbor's tree. The neighbor came running out with a pitchfork, and the boys ran off; some toward the town, my father toward the cemetery. There he saw two horses turning around a cross on a grave. He started to leave but the horses saw him and came after him. He came to a field where wheat had been harvested. He tripped and fell down. The horses were rearing up on him, kicking out with their hooves. He got up and fled again, making the sign of the cross with his tongue. The horses turned away, so he turned and pursued them with a big stick. The horses started turning somersaults and turned into two big mill stones and rolled booming into the valley and disappeared. My father went home. His father asked him what had hit him; he was bruised on the face and head. He remained ill for six weeks. The priest came and prayed over him.

4. Şanţ (B-Năsăud), July 28, 1977.

"Her father came upon a horse on the road and thought he'd ride it back to his village. But when he tried to catch it, to mount it, he couldn't.

He continued on foot, and the horse started following him. It followed him all the way to his house and then came up and bit him in the back, trapping his shirt. He fought with it and freed himself."

5. Corneiu (Cluj), Cluj Archives No. 2000 Ii, 1971.

"On the eve of Saint George's day a cart wheel appeared rolling through the village. Some boys ran after it and captured it. They took it and tied it up on a wall behind a house. Two days later the wheel was gone, but there was a woman hanging there. She was from a neighboring village. They knew her."

"A *strigoi* takes milk from cattle. *Pricolici* [were-wolves] don't."

III. Witches in the river:

1. Gura Rîului (Sibiu), June 20, 1977.

"When I was small in my parents' house, I took the cart and oxen out at 3:00 in the morning. I saw a woman bathing in the river just beyond the bridge. I was very afraid. I was small. I asked myself, 'What can that be?' The woman began to follow me. The oxen walked slowly. The woman followed saying, 'Hai, hai, duci-te' [Go go, get on with you]. The woman sat

down on a rock near the road, and I went off into the mountains. She wasn't from the village. Witches take milk from cows."

2. Tilişca (Sibiu), June 21, 1977.

"Near the mill I heard some splashing once late at night. I threw
a rock and saw the shape of a woman run off from the river.
What could that be at 12:00 at night?"

3. Tilişca (Sibiu), June 21, 1977.

"I saw a woman bathing in the river in winter; there was ice. I
said, 'Good evening.' She said, 'What you saw you didn't see.
Be off with you.'"

4. Tilişca (Sibiu), June 19, 1977.

"Some young men saw a young woman bathing in the river.
They grabbed her. The woman said, 'Tell nobody, or it will be
bad for you.'

The men said that they had seen a *strigoaica*, but didn't say
her name."

IV. The cow doesn't give milk:

1. Josenii-Bîrgăului (B-Năsăud), August 3, 1977.

"A cow didn't give milk any longer. It went to a neighbor's
house. It walked to that house to be milked. The neighbor was
a witch."

2. Sibiel (Sibiu), June 17, 1977.

"Our family cow wasn't giving any milk. My father-in-law took
some branches with hazel-nuts from the hazel tree and slapped
the back of the cow with them saying, 'I beat the witch, I beat
the witch.' Then they put a string before the cow and made
her walk over it. The teats came unblocked (they had been
dried up), and the milk came back."

3. Tilişca (Sibiu), June 19, 1977.

"I had a cow with wide teats and a good-sized udder, but it
wouldn't give milk. I went to a Saxon woman in Gîrbova [a
German village] and obtained a charm to cure the curse. The
reason the cow wouldn't give milk is the following. I came
back to my house one day and found the barn door unlocked,
even though I was sure I had locked it. I realized that somebody had been there, and had taken the cow's milk. This was
the charm. I took some garlic, money, and pork grease with
mold on it ['*o ţura rinceda*'] to the charmer. The Saxon woman
began a spell, and at exactly that moment, the cow began to
eat (a girl left with the cow confirmed the time of the cure). I

used the spoiled grease as an ointment. One night at midnight, my horse became frightened of something and broke out of the barn. The next morning the cow began to give milk."

V. Miscellaneous:

1. Hangu (Neamț), May 20, 1977.
"A boy in the village who had a tail was a witch. He became a respected property owner in the village."

2. Tilișca (Sibiu), June 21, 1977.
"A man in the mountains of Groapele took a black lamb, ripped out its heart, and put it in the fire and burned it. He mixed the cinders into the food of the other sheep. They became mad; they didn't give milk, and fled from one another. The shepherds found the man, and killed him."

3. Șanț (B-Năsăud), July 27, 1977.
"A child, a relative of mine, died, and was buried. One day his father saw that the grave had been stirred up. He uncovered the body and found that the fingers and toes had been cut off. The father told the priest who said that he'd take care of it the next Sunday at mass. That Sunday, the priest announced what had happened, and said whoever had committed the evil deed would die all alone, except for the company of big crows. Just then a woman fell down in the church and crows flew in and hovered over the body as she died."

VI. Vampires:

1. Sălcea (Broșteni), May 24, 1977.
"In my grandfather's family there were nine boys. The seventh, Visarion, died by drowning, and came back from the dead to haunt his family. Visarion's mother said he came back to haunt them, not to do harm. He made noises. They felt his presence until midnight."

2. Tilișca (Sibiu), June 21, 1977.
"A *strigoi* was disinterred and a nail plunged through its heart. The heart was not dead."

3. Șanț (Năsăud), July 28, 1977.
"A dead man who was killed by stabbing, and who had been buried would come back each night to look for his wife and daughter. Then he'd get back in his coffin, the lid would close, and off he'd go, like an automobile. Back into the grave.
The neighbors told him his family had moved away and he stopped coming back."

4. Holod (Bihor), August 5, 1977; (E 251.3.2)

"The notary of the town of Vîntere had a servant who was accused of taking milk from cows. He denied it and to prove his innocence he took off all his clothes and hid one night to see who was the guilty person.

He saw a *strigoaica* who came as a dog and sucked the milk from the cows. He jammed his pitchfork into the dog and it fled, and when it got back to its house, it died.

The priest of the village heard what had happened and called the servant to him. He told him to go and buy new clothes and to pay the first price asked. He told him also to bury the dead witch without a casket and to watch over the body for three nights.

The servant hired another man to help him. The first night the witch came out of the grave, but he hid behind the church cross, and she didn't find him. She looked and looked until 3:00 in the morning when she returned to the grave, weeping for not having found him.

The second night, two witches came out, but he hid behind the church altar. They didn't find him.

The third night three witches came out and looked and looked, and discovered him, but by then it was 3:00 and they had to go back to the grave.

He fled to his house and now he is married with children."

5. Marginea (Bihor), August 8, 1977.

"A young woman found her father dead one day, and she herself died. A young man from the village found her dead in her bed. The young man left the house and when he came back later she was sitting up in the bed.

The young man's mother forbid him to return to that house. The girl who was no longer dead married someone else from the village although she was in love with the first young man. The young man was in the fields one day when a wolf appeared in front of him, running back and forth like a dog with its master. The boy took a wooden stick and began to beat the wolf. The wolf fell to the ground and stayed there.

The next day the young girl was found in bed; her ribs were cracked. The boy was afraid; he knew she was the wolf and might kill him. The girl went to the hospital.

Soon after the young man was out in the fields. The wolf came to him and spoke to him. It reproached him saying that it could have hurt him before, but didn't, and now he had wounded her so badly she couldn't be a true woman." (That is, have children.)

APPENDIX D

LEGENDS OF DRAGONS AND FAIRIES

1. Gura Rîului (Sibiu), June 20, 1977.
   "I saw a dragon of eighty centimeters in length coming in a whirl-wind, on the edge of the town of Christian, flying about four meters off the ground. 'Where do they come from? From air currents, whirlwinds.'
   I don't think it was anything but the wind.
   If you put your foot in Lake Cindrelul, a dragon comes out. It once threw a rock into the lake, but nothing happened."
2. Tilişca (Sibiu), June 21, 1977.
   "I saw a large dragon (five meters long) in the mountains in Vîlcea. They have some connection with the Black Sea.
   On the feast of Saint Ilie (Elijah), there is a big festival of shepherds and sheep with dancing and drinking plum brandy. Once an elderly woman began to sing and lament, and related, weeping, how her son had died seven years previously. He had seen a big dragon and his dog had killed it. The dog died the same day. The dog was itself very big and strong. It had killed a bear the day they left to go up to the mountain with the sheep. The serpent wrapped itself around the dog and killed it, while the shepherd beat the thing on the head. Then the dog bit it. They buried the dragon that day, the day the dog died. And the same day the next year the son died."
3. Tilişca (Sibiu), June 19, 1977.
   "My father was going up the mountain to bring back wood one day when he saw a man dressed in black with a large book under his arm. The man stopped by a lake (Lake Cindrelu) and began reading in the book. He called out a dragon, and when it came out, mounted it, and they flew off. Rain and hail came. The man was a *solomonar* (sorcerer of storms and tempests). See: Thompson motif no. D 199.2.1., "Magician flies with dragon"; and, tale-type 326C, "Magician entices dragon from swamp.""

4. Tilişca (Sibiu), June 19, 1977.

"I saw another dragon with a woman directing it. Where she stood, the rain and hail didn't fall."

5. Tilişca (Sibiu), June 19, 1977.

"A big dragon fell to earth near Sibiu. It fell under a bridge, and many, many people came to look at it. It happened about fifteen years ago."

6. Tilişca (Sibiu), June 21, 1977.

"There was a town of Greabla. When people were at the church a dragon came and surrounded, entwined the church with its head locked on its tail. The people opened the windows and escaped. The whole town moved to a new place called Grebeşti."

7. Sibiel (Sibiu), June 17, 1977.

"One night my father was sleeping on the porch of his house. He heard the song of the *iele* (fairies) inviting him to come and make them some bricks. He refused saying he had to take care of his animals. He never again slept on the porch."

APPENDIX E

BELIEFS CONCERNING WERE-WOLVES AND VAMPIRES: FOLK MYTHOLOGY

1. The reason for the existence of were-wolves (*Pricolici, tricolici, strigoi de lup*):
   1. They have a little tail (*coada*):
      Şanţ (B-Năsăud) — 4 respondents
      Josenii-Bîrgăului (B-Năsăud) — 2 respondents
      Forosig (Bihor) — 1 respondent
      Leşu (B-Năsăud) — 1 respondent
      Vîrciorog (Bihor) — 4 respondents
      Rod (Sibiu) — 1 respondent
      Săvineşti-de-Sus (Neamţ) — 1 respondent
   2. They were weaned and then let return to the breast:
      Şanţ (B-Năsăud) - 4 respondents
      Lesu (B-Năsăud) — 2 respondents
      Josenii-Bîrgăului (B-Năsăud) — 2 respondents
   3. They were pre-destined from birth; also as a curse and punishment:
      Şanţ (B-Năsăud) — 2 respondents
      Josenii-Bîrgăului (B-Năsăud) — 1 respondent
      Vîrciorog (Bihor) — 1 respondent
      Gura Riului (Sibiu) — 1 respondant
      Tilişca (Sibiu) — 1 respondent
   4. They were born with the caul; it can't be broken until the appro-
      priate destiny is spoken, e.g., "a witch for milk, a witch for poverty,
      a witch for music, a witch for weaving, a witch for cooking. . .":
      Suiug (Bihor) — 1 respondent
   5. They were born with fur down the front of the body:
      Josenii-Bîrgăului (B-Năsăud) — 1 respondent
   6. They were the third or fourth generation of illegitimate children:
      Sibiel (Sibiu) — 1 respondent
      Răşinari (Sibiu) — 2 respondents
   7. They were the seventh child of all male children:
      Jina (Sibiu) — 1 respondent
   8. They were born with "wild" or bad blood; with evil spirits:
      Josenii-Bîrgăului (B-Năsăud) — 1 respondent
      Forosig (Bihor) — 1 respondent

II. Children conceived on the eve of high religious holidays will be
born with deformities-"animal characteristics"—will be unlucky,
or malicious:
Şanţ (B-Năsăud) — 2 respondents
Lesu (B-Năsăud) — 2 respondents
Josenii-Bîrgăului (B-Năsăud) — 1 respondent
Ştupca (Neamţ) — 1 respondent
Sălcea (Botoşani) — 1 respondent
Trusești (Botoşani) — 1 respondent
Buhalniţa (Neamţ) — 1 respondent
Huiduman (Neamţ) — 1 respondent
Hangu (Neamţ) — 1 respondent
Schit (Neamţ) — 1 respondent
Grintieşul (Neamţ) — 1 respondent

III. What the were-wolves do:
1. On the eve of high religious holidays, they prowl and attack
people:
Şanţ (B-Năsăud) — 6 respondents
Lesu (B-Năsăud) — 1 respondent
Josenii-Bîrgăului (B-Năsăud) — 1 respondent
2. They attack people, especially those with whom they have quar-
reled; at night between 12:00 and 3:00:
Lesu (B-Năsăud) — 1 respondent
Josenii-Bîrgăului (B-Năsăud) — 2 respondents
Hidişelu-de-Sus (Bihor) — 1 respondent
Sibiel (Sibiu) — 1 respondent
3. They prowl at night with other dogs; especially when dogs are
in heat:
Rod (Sibiu) — 1 respondent
Gura Rîului (Sibiu) — 2 respondents
Răşinari (Sibiu) — 1 respondent
4. They prowl at night, attacked by *real* dogs:
Tilişca (Sibiu) — 2 respondents
Răşinari (Sibiu) — 1 respondent
5. Prowl at night:
Josenii-Bîrgăului (B-Năsăud) — 1 respondent
Răşinari (Sibiu) — 1 respondent
6. Eat cattle or sheep:
Holod (Bihor) — 1 respondent
Vîrciorog (Bihor) — 2 respondents

7. Take milk from cattle:
   Holod (Bihor), — 1 respondent
   Suiug (Bihor) — 1 respndent
8. The were-wolf was also a robber and crook:
   Sibiel (Sibiu) — 1 respondent
9. The were-wolf cannot rest until made to bleed:
   Tilişca (Aibiu) — 1 respondent

IV. Attitudes toward were-wolves.
   1. They don't exist any more; people are wiser, better behaved:
      Leşu (B-Năsăud) — 1 respondent
      Şanţ (B-Năsăud) — 1 respondent
      Gura Rîullui (Sibiu) — 1 respondent
   2. People are careful about them, but there is no scandal, no per-
      secution; they are allowed by God, and are treated just like
      everyone else:
      Forosig (Bihor) — 1 respondent
      Holod (Bihor) — 1 respondent
      Tilişca (Sibiu) — 2 respondents
      Sibiel (Sibiu) — 1 respondent
   3. It is the result of a curse, a punishment:
      Sibiel (Sibiu) — 1 respondent
      Răşinari (Sibiu) — 1 respondent
      Suiug (Bihor) — 1 respondent
   4. They don't know they are were-wolves:
      Sibiel (Sibiu) — 1 respondent
   5. They are a kind of witch (*strigoi*):
      Tilişca (Sibiu) — 1 respondent

V. The mode of transformation to the animal:
   1. By turning three somersaults:
      Forosig (Bihor) — 1 respondent
      Holod (Bihor) — 1 respondent
      Hidişul-de-Sus (Bihor) — 1 respondent
      Vîrciorog (Bihor) — 2 respondents
      Marginea (Bihor) — 1 respondent
   2. By turning nine somersaults:
      Marginea (Bihor) — 1 respndent
   3. By turning somersaults:
      Leşu (B-Năsăud) — 2 respondents
      Şanţ (B-Năsăud) — 1 respondent

Suiug (Bihor — 1 respondent
Marginea (Bihor) — 1 respondent
Tilişca (Sibiu) — 2 respondents
Sibiel (Sibiu) — 2 respondents
4. "Night is their time."
   Răşinari (Sibiu) — 1 respondent
   Gura Rîului (Sibiu) — 1 respondent

VI. Tranformation to human form: (D 712.6 "Disenchantment by wounding.");
   1. If made to bleed, it is forced to regain human form:
      Şanţ (B-Năsăud) — 3 respondents
      Josenii-Bîrgăului (B-Năsăud) — 1 respondent
      Marginea (Bihor) — 1 respondent
      Tilişca (Sibiu) — 2 respondents
      Sibiel (Sibiu) — 1 respndent
      Gura Rîului (Sibiu) — 2 respondents
      Răşinari (Sibiu) —1 respondent
   2. If made to bleed, this breaks the enchantment, and he stays a man; cannot rest unless made to bleed:
      Răşinari (Sibiu) — 1 respondent
      Tilişca (Sibiu) — 1 respondent

VII. The reason for the existence of witches/vampires (*strigoi vi/strigi mort*):
   1. They have a little tail (*coda*):
      Şanţ (B-Năsăud) — 2 respondents
      Holod (Bihor) — 2 respondents
      Vîrciorog (Bihor) — 1 respondent
      Suiug (Bihor) — 2 respondents
      Marginea (Bihor) — 2 respondents
      Tilişca (Sibiu) — 4 respondents
      Sibiel (Sibiu) —1 respondent
      Hangu (Neamţ) — 1 respondent
      Dreptu (Neamţ) — 1 respondent
      Săvineşti-de-Sus (Neamţ) — 1 respondent
      Schiţ (Neamţ) — 1 respondent
      Cornu Lunchi (Suceava) — 1 respondent
      Ştupca (Suceava) — 1 respondent
      Sălcea (Botoşani) — 1 respondent
      Truseşti (Botoşani) — 1 respondent

2. Born with the caul:
   Suiug (Bihor) — 1 respondent
3. Weaned and let return to the breast:
   Șanț (B-Năsăud) — 1 respondent
4. Have fur down the back:
   Șanț (B-Năsăud) — 1 respondent
5. The seventh child:
   Cornu Lunchi (Suceava) — 1 respondent
   Capu Codrului (Suceava) — 1 respondent
   Ilisești (Suceava) — 1 respondent
   Sălcea (Botoșani) — 1 respondent
6. The seventh of all female children:
   Trusești (Botoșani) — 1 respondent
7. Third generation illegitimate child:
   Sibiel (Sibiu) — 2 respondents
8. Illegitimate, unbaptized child that dies:
   Josenii-Bîrgăului (B-Năsăud) — 1 respondent
9. It is a curse or punishment from God:
   Suiug (Bihor) — 1 respondent
   Sibiel (Sibiu) — 2 respondents
   Tilișca (Sibiu) — 1 respondent
10. A cat or other animal crossed over the deceased before burial:
    Bîila (Vlașca) — 1 respondent

VIII. What the witches and vampires do:
   1. They take the milk from cattle or sheep: (E 251.3.2 "Vampires milk cows dry")
      Șanț (B-Năsăud) — 1 respondent
      Josenii-Bîrgăului (B-Năsăud) — 3 respondents
      Forosig (Bihor) — 1 respondent
      Holod (Bihor) — 1 respondent
      Vîrciogor (Bihor) — 1 respondent
      Suiug (Bihor) — 3 respondents
      Marginea (Bihor) — 1 respondent
      Tilișca (Sibiu) — 6 respondents
      Sibiel (Sibiu) — 2 respondents
      Jina (Sibiu) — 2 respondents
      Gura Rîului (Sibiu) — 2 respondents
      Rășinari (Sibiu) — 1 respondent

2. If the milk is depleted then blood is drawn from cattle and sheep:
   Tilişca (Sibiu) — 2 respondents
3. They stick a pitchfork into the ceiling and draw the milk:
   Tilişca (Sibiu) — 1 respondent
4. They change into a cat and suck the milk from cows:
   Marginea (Bihor) — 1 respondent
5. They take the life energy from wheat; the life force from animals:
   Suiug (Bihor) — 1 respondent
   Schit (Neamţ) — 1 respondent
6. They prowl on the eve of Saint Andrew's feast day until 12:00, until the cock-crow:
   Farcaşa (Neamţ) — 1 respondent
   Săvineşti-de-Sus (Neamţ) — 1 respondent
   Schit (Neamţ) — 1 respondent
   Bradu (Neamţ) — 1 respondent
   Pipirig (Neamţ) — 2 respondents
   Cornu Lunchi (Suceava) — 1 respondent
   Sălcea (Botoşani) — 1 respondent
   Truseşti (Botoşani) — 1 respondent
7. The eve of Saint Andrew's feast day is a carnival of the dead; unbaptized children weep at their parents' graves, those who did evil in their lifetime are condemned to do it after; they kill people:
   Farcaşa (Neamţ) — 1 respondent
8. The witch flies on a broomstick; can deform people she meets:
   Pipirig (Neamţ) — 1 respondent
9. They kill people who see them:
   Tilişca (Sibiu) — 1 respondent
10. They come out of the grave and eat sheep and cattle:
    Marginea (Bihor) — 1 respondent
11. They prowl at night:
    Şanţ (B-Năsăud) — 1 respondent
    Rod (Sibiu) — 1 respondent
12. They bathe in the river at night or in winter:
    Tilişca (Sibiu) — 3 respondents
    Gura Rîului (Sibiu) — 1 respondent
    Răşinari (Sibiu) — 1 respondent
13. They don't eat garlic:
    Huiduman (Neamţ) — 1 respondent
    Dreptu (Neamţ) — 1 respondent

14. They come out of the river after death:
   Tilişca (Sibiu) — 1 respondent
15. They do not harm anyone or anything:
   Gura Rîului (Sibiu) — 1 respondent
   Hangu (Neamţ) — 1 respondent
   Dreptu (Neamţ) — 1 respondent
16. They don't change into an animal form:
   Bradu (Neamţ) — 1 respondent

IX. Attitudes toward the witches and vampires:
1. There are many kinds of *strigoi*; for weaving, cooking, milk, making money, charming women, charming wolves, dogs, hares:
   Suiug (Bihor) — 1 respondent
   Marginea (Bihor) — 2 respondents
   Jina (Sibiu)   1 respondent
   Holod (Bihor) — 1 respondent
2. People fear them, but don't persecute them:
   Tilişca (Sibiu) — 3 respondents
   Farcaşa (Neamţ) — 1 respondent
   Schit (Neamţ) — 1 respondent
3. They're not as prevalent now; people don't make as much of them; there are just stories:
   Marginea (Bihor) — 1 respondent
   Tilişca (Sibiu) — 2 respondents
   Gura Rîului (Sibiu) — 2 respondents
   Rod (Sibiu) — 1 respondent
   Răşinari (Sibiu) — 1 respondent
4. They are just like other people; they are treated as such:
   Gura Rîului (Sibiu) — 2 respondents
   Holod (Sibiu) — 1 respondent
5. Nobody knows anything for sure; we haven't seen them:
   Jina (Sibiu) — 1 respondent
6. One doesn't reveal the witches' identity:
   Tilişca (Sibiu) — 2 respondents
7. People who are born with a little tail have a connection with the Devil; Satan is the leader of the witches and vampires:
   Josenii-Bîrgăului (B-Năsăud) — 1 respondent
   Suiug (Bihor) — 1 respondent
8. Vampires cannot remain in the earth:
   Suiug (Bihor) — 1 respondent
9. Every man has two natures, demonic and divine:
   Forosig (Bihor) — 1 respondent

10. They have extraordinary strength and will power:
    Jina (Sibiu) — 1 respondent

X. Protective Countermeasures:
  1. Rub garlic on the windows, doors, and animals in the form of a cross on the eve of Saint Andrew's feast day; take some along in your pocket when venturing out:
     Fărcaşa (Neamţ) — 1 respondent
     Schit (Neamţ) — 1 respondent
     Grinţiesul (Neamţ) — 1 respondent
     Bradu (Neamţ) — 1 respondent
     Boroaia (Suceava) — 1 respondent
     Ştupca (Suceava) — 1 respondent
  2. Rub garlic or *ordolean* on the doors, windows, or on the door jamb, or eat garlic—anytime:
     Pipirig (Neamţ) — 1 respondent
     Sălcea (Botoşani) — 1 respondent
     Truseşti (Botoşani) — 1 respondent
     Bivolar (Iaşi) — 1 respondent
     Rod (Sibiu) — 1 respondent
  3. White witches (*vrăjitori*) use magic to counteract the witch:
     Sibiel (Sibiu) — 1 respondent
     Tilişca (Sibiu) — 1 respondent
  4. Drive a nail or stake through the heart of a suspected vampire, if there is blood, the vampire is destroyed; especially if the body is lying face down:
     Sibiel (Sibiu) — 1 respondent
     Suiug (Bihor) — 1 respondent
  5. Rub garlic on the doors and on the cows on the eve of Saint George's feast day:
     Forosig (Bihor) — 1 respondent
  6. Rub *leuştean* on the forehead of the cattle before taking them out to pasture on the eve of Saint John's feast day (June 24, the summer solstice):
     Gura Rîului (Sibiu) — 1 respondent
  7. Turn the dead body over in the coffin to prevent it from leaving the grave:
     Jina (Sibiu) — 1 respondent
  8. Reverse the mirrors in the house of the deceased before burial:
     Bîila (Ilfov) — 1 respondent
  9. Have the priest say prayers against a witch's enchantment:
     Jina (Sibiu) — 1 respondent

10 Distribute garlic at church on Easter; whoever doesn't eat it is a witch or vampire:
   Marginea (Bihor) — 1 respondent
11. Disenchantment is possible:
   Forosig (Bihor) — 1 respondent
12. Make the sign of the cross, the vampire will disappear:
   Suiug (Bihor) — 1 respondent

APPENDIX F

WOLF, ANIMAL, AND MISCELLANEOUS RELIGIOUS BELIEFS

I. Wolf Beliefs:
1. Saint Peter is the patron of wolves; they are his "dogs" (pets):
   Tilişca (Sibiu) — 4 respondents
   Gura Rîului (Sibiu) — 2 respondents
2. Saint Peter, Saint Andrew and Saint Philip are the patrons of the wolves:
   Leşu (B-Năsăud) — 1 respondent
3. Saint Andrew is the patron of the wolves:
   Fărcaşa (Neamţ) — 1 respondent
   Săvineşti-de-Sus (Neamţ) — 1 respondent
   Schit (Neamţ) — 1 respondent
   Bradu (Neamţ) — 1 respondent
   Pipirig (Neamţ) — 1 respondent
   Bucharest — 1 respondent
4. Unless one abstains from meat or gives alms to the poor on Saint Peter's feast day, he will send the wolves to kill the farm animals:
   Tilişca (Sibiu) — 3 respondents
   Gura Rîului (Sibiu) — 2 respondents
5. One must abstain from meat on Saint George's feast day so that the wolves will not come and eat the cattle and sheep:
   Schit (Neamţ) — 1 respondent
6. Women must abstain from sewing and needle work on the eve of Saint Andrew's feast day, lest he give the wolves permission to eat the farm animals:
   Săvineşti-de-Sus (Neamţ) — 1 respondent
7. The wolves howl on Saint Peter's day for something to eat:
   Jina (Sibiu) — 1 respondent
8. On the eve of Saint George's feast day, Saint Andrew gives the wolves permission to eat certain animals:
   Schit (Neamţ) — 1 respondent

9. The wolf who is surprised by the rising sun with his mouth closed cannot eat any animals that day; if open, it must find a victim:
Leşu (Năsăud) — 1 respondent
Jina (Sibiu) — 1 respondent
Răşinari (Sibiu) — 1 respondent
Tilişca (Sibiu) — 1 respondent

10. The seventh or ninth wolf cub is not a wolf at all but a lynx; it crawls through the cow's vagina into the stomach and devours the insides:
Dreptu (Neamţ) - 1 respondent
Poiana Rechiţa (Ncamţ) — 1 respondent
Săvineşti-de-Sus (Neamţ) — 1 respondent
Bradu (Neamţ) — 1 respondent

11. The last wolf cub is a lynx:
Pipirig (Neamţ) — 1 respondent

12. By casting a spell and blowing through a wolf's gullet, you can accomplish what you want, make a marriage for your children, cure your son of fearing, do harm to someone:
Biila (Ilfov) — 1 respondent
Şanţ (B-Năsăud) — 1 respondent

13. Pulverized ashes of wolf bones is a good remedy for skin ailments:
Biila (Ilfov) — 1 respondent

14. An evil or hard person is said to have the fur of the wolf:
Grinţieşul (Neamţ) — 1 respondent

15. The wolf will kill all the sheep, but eat only one:
Răşinari (Sibiu) — 1 respondent

16. Rub garlic on the doors of the animal shed to keep wolves away:
Schit (Neamţ) — 1 respondent

17. The shepherds catch a wolf and put a spell on it "leaga gura lupului," ["they bind the mouth of the wolf"] to protect the sheep from wolves:
Bistricioara (Neamţ) — 1 respondent

II. Animal Beliefs:
1. One should not embroider or sew or loom on Wednesdays or Fridays, or it will be bad for your animals:
Tilişca (Sibiu) — 1 respondent

2. A toad cooked in sheeps' butter and fed to the sheep will protect them from flies and the sores that attract flies:
Tilişca (Sibiu) — 1 respondent

3. Cut off a serpent's head and fill the mouth with garlic; bury it, when the garlic has sprouted, dig it up and put it on your cap; with it you can see who is a witch or vampire:
Sibiel (Sibiu) — 1 respondent

4. August 1 is the special day for bears; ("Babu Nicolae"):
Tilişca (Sibiu) — 1 respondent

5. March 9 is the special day for ants:
Bucharest — 1 respondent

6. On the eve of Saint George's feast day, the animals speak:
Ştupca (Suceava) — 1 respondent

III. Religious Beliefs:

1. The child born on Easter, Christmas, Pentecost is blessed by God:
Buhalniţa (Neamţ) — 1 respondent
Huiduman (Neamţ) — 1 respondent
Tilişca (Sibiu) — 2 respondents

2. Death on Easter brings immediate immortality (heaven):
Răşinari (Sibiu) — 1 respondent
Buhalniţa (Neamţ) — 1 respondent
Dreptu (Neamţ) — 1 respondent
Fărcaşa (Neamţ) — 1 respondent

3. Death in Holy Week means a life of great sinning; death after Easter, straight to heaven:
Neamţ Monastery — 1 respondent

4. Born with the caul signifies future importance and good fortune:
Tilişca (Sibiu) — 1 respondent
Rod (Sibiu) — 1 respondent

5. The caul is related to the *Ursitoare* [the goddesses of destiny] :
Suiug (Bihor) — 1 respondent

6. Saint Elijah (Ilie) whips and chases the devils with lightning in his cart of thunder:
Tilişca (Sibiu) — 1 respondent

7. On Saint Andrew's feast day, the sky opens and the good can see heaven:
Ştupca (Suceava) — 1 respondent

IV. Miscellaneous:

1. The hours between 11:00 p.m. and 1:00 a.m. are the "evil hours" (*ceasuri rele*):
Tilişca (Sibiu) — 1 respondent

2. Concerning the *Ursitoare* [the goddess of destiny] , people say such things are foolish and worthless:
   Tilișca (Sibiu) — 1 respondent

3. If it is raining and the sun is out the witches are bathing:
   Rășinari (Sibiu) — 1 respondent

4. After giving birth, the mother must touch nothing for three days, until the priest blesses and absolves. Otherwise the child will be damned:
   Buhalnița (Neamț) — 1 respondent

5. The seventh child is very intelligent:
   Fărcașa (Neamț) — 1 respondent

6. Man is a clay pot (*oala*), his body must be broken for his spirit to go to heaven:
   Bucharest — 1 respondent

7. Children who die unbaptized prowl like shadows; say some prayers and they disappear:
   Forosig (Bihor) — 1 respondent

8. Unbaptized, abandoned infants eat the moon and cause eclipses; they are called *vîrcolacul*: (A 737.1 "Eclipse caused by were-wolf.")
   Brănești (Ilfov) — 2 respondents

9. If Saint Peter's feast day falls on a Wednesday or a Friday, the sheep will not have good milk, since Wednesday and Friday are already fast days, i.e., days of abstinence:
   Gura Rîului (Sibiu) — 1 respondent

10. Children born with a little tail must have an operation; it is just chance, like a lamb born with two heads:
    Forosig (Bihor) — 1 respondent

NOTES

CHAPTER II: SOCIAL STABILITY

1. *Strigoi* is the Romanian word for "witch," "wizard," "ghost," or "reanimated dead" (vampire). It derives from the verb *a striga*, "to cry or to shriek," and from the Latin *striga*, "witch," and *strix*, "demon birds that suck human blood." "Vampire" is virtually non-existent in Romania; it comes from the Turkish, according to the Oxford English Dictionary, 1928, and entered western Europe by way of Yugoslavia and Hungary. *Nosferatu* is an archaic Romanian word meaning "the Devil" which I have not encountered personally in Romania.

2. For previous research, see Harry Senn, "Some Were-wolf Legends and the *Călușari* Ritual in Romania," *East European Quarterly*, 11, No. 1 (1977), 1-14, and "Were-Beings and *Strigoi* Legends in Village Life: Romanian Folk Beliefs," *East European Quarterly*, 14, No. 3 (1980), 303-314.

3. Edward Evans-Pritchard, *Witchcraft, Oracles and Magic among the Azande* (Oxford: Clarendon Press, 1937); Max Marwick, *Sorcery in its Social Setting: A Study of the Northern Rhodesian Cewu* (Manchester: Manchester University Press, 1965). I am indebted to Mary Douglas for the preceding overview in *Witchcraft Confessions and Accusations*, Mary Douglas, editor (London: Tavistock Publications, 1970), pp. xvi-xviii.

4. William Morgan, *Human Wolves among the Navaho*, Yale University Publications in Anthropology, no. 11 (New Haven: Yale University Press, 1936), p. 12.

5. Ernest Jones, *Nightmare, Witches and Devils* (New York, 1931), p. 148, 150, 151.

6. Clyde Kluckhohn and Dorothea Leighton, *The Navaho* (Garden City, New York: Doubleday, (1962), p. 187.

7. Douglas, *Confessions*, p. xxxv.

8. Claude Levi-Strauss, *L'Origine des manières de table*. Mythologiques III (Paris: Plon, 1968), p. 422.

9. R. G. Lienhardt, "Some Notions of Witchcraft among the Dinka," *Africa*, 21, No. 4 (1951), 317-318.

10. Malcolm Ruel, "Were-animals and the Introverted Witch," in *Witchcraft Confessions and Accusations*, Mary Douglas, editor, pp. 333-350, p. 344.

11. See Sigmund Freud: "An uncanny experience occurs either when infantile complexes which have been repressed are once more revived by some impression, or when primitive beliefs which have been surmounted seem once more to be confirmed." *The Uncanny*, Complete Works, XVII (London: The Hogarth Press, 1955), p. 249.

12. Wilhelm Hertz, *Der Werwolf* (Stuttgart, 1862), p. 56.

13. Jaan Puhvel, "Hittite *hurkis* and *hurkel*," *Die Sprache*, 17 (1971), 42-45, p. 44.

14. Heinrich Brunner, *Deutsche Rechtsgeschichte*, 2nd ed. (Leipzig: 1906), I, 234; cited by Mary Gerstein, "Germanic Warg: The Outlaw as Werewolf" in *Myth in Indo-European Antiquity*, Gerald James Larson, ed. (Berkeley: University of California Press, 1974), p. 131, to whom I am indebted for the general ideas on were-wolves and outlaws.

15. The Franks: *Lex Salica*, title 58; *Lex Ripuaria*, title 87; for the Normans, Frederic Pluquet, *Contes populaires, préjugés, patois, proverbes*. (Caen, 1834), p. 15; for the Anglo-Saxons, the *Laws of Canute*, titles 7 and 3. These cites are found in Kirby F. Smith, "An Historical Study of the Werewolf in Literature," *PMLA*, 9 (1894), p. 26, and in Sabine Baring-Gould, *The Book of Were-wolves* (London: Smith Elder & Co., 1865), p, 48.

16. Mary Gerstein, "Outlaw as Werewolf," p. 135, 143.

17. Mircea Eliade lists them as the Dacians, the Hyrcanoi, the Orkoi, the Lycaones of Arcadia, the Lucani, and the Hirpini; Romulus and Remus were sons of the wolf-god Mars and suckled by a she-wolf; the people of Genghis Khan are also included here; *Zalmoxis The Vanishing God* (Chicago: University of Chicago Press, 1972), p. 1, 4. See also: Robert Eisler, *Man into Wolf* (London: Routledge & Kegan Paul Ltd., 1951), p. 33. Eisler further underscores the great number of Italic, Germanic, and Greek personal names that mean "wolf," and speculates that were-wolf beliefs and wolf names derive from the deep emotional upheaval of the historical transition from fruit gathering herds of "finders" to carnivorous hunters. (p. 33) Romanian scholars Eliade and Octavian Buhociu ascribe the wolf syndrome of ritual and brotherhoods to pastoral societies, as represented by Romania, incorporating in sacred rites behavior of preceding, hunting tribes; Eliade, *Zalmoxis*, Buhociu, *Die Rumänische Volkskultur und Ihre Mythologie* (Wiesbaden, Otto Harrassowitz, 1974).

18. Eliade, *Zalmoxis*, p. 7, 11.

19. Stig Wikander, *Der Arische Männerbund* (Lund, 1938), p. 64, 65; see also, George Widengren, *Hochgottglauge im alten Iran* (Uppsala, 1938), pp. 342-344.

20. Herodotus of Halcarnassus, Fourth Book, *Melpomena*, cited by P. M. Schuhl, *Essai sur la formation de la pensée grecque* (Paris: 1934), p. 79ff, and by Montague Summers, *The Werewolf* (London: Kegan Paul, 1933), p. 133.

21. "Thrace," and "Getae," *Encyclopedia Brittanica*.

22. Eliade, *Zalmoxis*, pp. 3-4.

23. See: Vasile Pârvan, *Getica, o protohistorie a Daciei* (Bucharest: 1926), pp. 519ff.

24. A. Nour, *Credințe, Rituri și Superstiții Geto-Dace* (Bucharest: Tipografia Cărților Bisericești, 1941), p. 66.

25. Diodorus of Sicily, *Historical Library*, F. M. Saltei and H. L. Edwards, eds., volume I (Oxford: Oxford University Press), p. 881.

26. Wallis Budge, *Osiris and the Egyptian Resurrection*, 1911, volume II, p. 159, 316.

27. A. B. Cook, *Zeus*, 1915, volume I, p. 99.

28. Hertz, *Der Werwolf*, p. 42.

29. Pliny, *Natural History* VIII, Plato, *Republic* VIII, Pausanias, VIII, are all cited by Jean Przluski, "Les Confréries de loup-garous dans les sociétés indo-européennes," *Revue de l'Histoire des Religions*, 121 (1940), 128-145, p. 29.

30. Georges Dumézil, *The Destiny of the Warrior* (Chicago: University of Chicago Press, 1970), p. 141; see also Dumézil, *Mythes et dieux des Germains* (Paris, 1939), p. 82. See further, Lily Weiser, *Altgermanische Junglingsweihen und Männerbunde* (Baden, 1927), and Otto Hofler, *Geheimbunde der Germanen* (Frankfurt a.M., 1934), I.

31. Mircea Eliade, *Rites and Symbols of Initiation* (New York: Harper Torchbooks, 1965), p. 72.

32. Dumézil, *The Destiny of the Warrior*, p. 142.

33. Eliade, *Zalmoxis*, p. 8. 18.

34. J. C. Lawson, *Modern Greek Folklore and Ancient Greek Religion* (New Hyde Park, New York: University Books, 1964), p. 384.

35. At. M. Marinescu, "Pricolicii," *Familia*, anul VIII (1872), p. 116.

36. John Fiske, *Myths and Mythmakers* (New York: Houghton Mifflin Co., 1914), p. 79.

37. Augustine, *De Civitate Dei* XXII, 22; *Contra Julianum*, VI, xxi, 67; cited in Peter Brown, "Sorcery, Demons and the Rise of Christianity from Late Antiquity into the Middle Ages," in *Witchcraft Confessions and Accusations*, p. 28.

38. Edward B. Tylor, *Primitive Culture*, vol. I (London: John Murray, 1871), p. 282.

39. Peter Brown, "Sorcery," p. 33.

40. Norman Cohn, "The Myth of Satan and His Human Servants," in *Witchcraft Confessions and Accusations*, p. 9.

41. Hertz, *Der Werwolf*, p. 96.

42. Jean Marx, *L'Inquisition en Dauphiné: étude sur le développement et la répression de l'hérésie et de la sorcellerie du XIVe au début du règne de François Ier* (Paris: H. Champion, 1914), p. 10: "ils croyaient fermement que . . . le diable était le chef de l'armée impie des sorciers . . . adonnée au mal et célébrant le sabbat . . . . Lorsque . . . face à face avec un certain développement des croyances magiques et superstitions populaires, la rencontre de la conception abstraite des juges avec la réalité concrète des croyances paysannes déclencha la répression."

43. Carlo Ginzburg, *I benandanti: Richerche sulla stregoneria et sui culti agrari tra cinquecento e seicento* (Turin, 1966), p. 8-9; cited in Mircea Eliade, *Occultism, Witchcraft and Cultural Fashions* (Chicago: University of Chicago Press, 1976), p. 73ff.

44. Ernest Jones, *Nightmare*, p. 237.

45. Ştefan Andreescu, *Vlad Ţepeş (Dracula) Intre Legendă şi Istoric* (Bucharest: Editura Minerva, 1976), p. 156.

46. Raymond T. McNally and Radu Florescu's entertaining and ingenious *In Search of Dracula* (Greenwich, Connecticut: New York Graphic Society, 1972) which studied the historical personage and blended in some folk beliefs concerning vampires generally confused this particular issue.

47. *Teutonic Mythology*, vol. III (London: George Bell & Sons, 1883), p. 1139.

48. R. Bleichsteiner, "Masken und Fastnachtsbrauche bei den Volkern des Kaukasus," *Oesterreichische Zeitschrift für Volkskunde*, n.s., 6 (1952), 18ff.

CHAPTER III: ROMANIAN WERE-WOLVES

1. The legends are part of my field collections gathered in two six-month periods in 1975 and 1977 with the assistance of grants from the Council for the International Exchange of Scholars (Fulbright) and the International Research and Exchanges Board (IREX), respectively.

2. Roman Jakobson, *Slavic Epic Studies*, Selected Writings 4, (Paris: Mouton & Co., 1966), p. 345.

3. Louis C. Jones, "Italian Werewolves," *New York Folklore Quarterly*, 6 (1950), 135, 136; Montague Summers, *The Werewolf* (London: Kegan Paul & Co., Ltd., p. 163.

4. See Horia Barbu Oprișan, *Monografia Folklorică a Teleormanului* (Bucharest: Casa Creației Populare a Teleormanului, 1971), pp. 251-256.

5. "Slavic Folklore," *Standard Dictionary of Folklore and Mythology* (New York: Funk and Wagnalls, 1972), p. 1020.

6. . Claude Gaignebet & Marie-Claude Florentin, *Le Carnaval* (Paris: Payot, 1974), p. 29.

7. Roman Jakobson, *Slavic Epic Studies*, p. 349.

8. "All Souls' Day," *Standard Dictionary of Folklore and Mythology*, p. 38.

9. James G. Frazer, *Ovid's Fasti* (London: Loeb Classical Library, 1951), p. 59.

10. Ernest Jones, *Nightmare, Witches and Devils* (New York, 1931), p. 136.

11. Guolart, *Thresor des histoires admirables et memorables de nostre temps* (n.p.: n.p., 1600), I, 336; cited in Jones, *Nightmare*, p. 136.

12. J. C. Lawson, *Modern Greek Folklore and Ancient Greek Religion* (New Hyde Park, New York: University Books, 1964), p. 228-229; Oskar Seyffert, *Dictionary of Classical Antiquities*, revised and edited by Henry Nettleship and J. E. Sandys (New York: Meridian Books, 1962), p. 190.

13. Seyffert, *Dictionary*, p. 190.

14. Karl Otfied Muller & John William Donaldson, *History of the Literature of Ancient Greece* (London: J. W. Parker & Son, 1858), I, 382.

15. Lawson, *Modern Greek Folklore*, p. 229, 192.

16. Bernhard Schmidt, *Das Volkslegender Neugriechen* (Leipzig, 1871), I, 142 & 147.

17. Octavian Buhociu, *Die Rumänische Volkskultur und ihre Mythologie* (Wiesbaden: Otto Harrassowitz, 1974), p. 72.

18. Wilhelm Hertz, *Der Werwolf* (Stuttgart, 1862), p. 120.

19. Georges Dumézil, *Le problème des centaures* (Paris: Librairie Orientaliste Paul Geuthner, 1929), p. 13: "à la fois redoutés et honorés, font fuir et font rire, voient les hommes trembler et sont aspergés d'avoine par les filles." Svatava Jakobson, "Slavic Folklore," *Standard Dictionary of Folklore and Mythology*.

20. E. T. Kirby, "The Origin of the Mummers' Play," *Journal of American Folklore*, 84 (1971), 275-288.

21. Violet Alford, *Pyrenean Festivals* (London: Chatto & Windus, 1937), p. 42-43; Alford and Rodney Gallop, *The Traditional Dance* (London: Methuen & Co., 1935), p. 74.

22. Simion Florian Marian, *Şărbătorile la Români* (Bucharest, 1889), II, 40ff.

23. Elisabeta Moldoveanu-Nestor, "Şărbătoare a seceresului," *Revista de Etnografia şi Folclor* (1964), p. 627.

24. Richard Volfram, "Alterklassen und Männerbunde in Rumänien," *Mitteilungen der Antrhopologischen Gesellschaft in Wien*, 44 (1934), 112ff.

25. Mircea Eliade, *Zalmoxis The Vanishing God* (Chicago: University of Chicago Press, 1972), p. 251.

26. For a general study of the ballad/hymn, see Adrian Fochi, *Miorița: Tipologie, circulaţie, geneză, texte, cu un studio introductiv de Pavel Apostol* (Bucharest, 1964); Mircea Eliade, in his extensive study of the ballad (*Zalmoxis*, pp. 226-256), lists the following sources of the text: I. Amzulescu, *Balade populare româneşti* (Bucharest, 1964), II, 463-486; I, 5-100; also by Amzulescu, "Cântecul nostru bătrânesc," *Revista de Folclor*, 5 (1960), 25-58; Petru Iroaie, "Miorița o il canto della fusione con la Natura," *Folklore*, 12 (Naples, 1958), 34-42. The distinction between ballad and carol relates to the restricted period of the year when the *colind* is sung, that is, the Christmas season, and the accompanying ritual and costumes. The ballad is thus a story in verse put to music which can be performed singly and at any time of the year—like a folktale.

27. Buhociu, *Mythologie*, p. 102: "Als Elemente mit magischer Funktion, die Gesundheit und Reichtum bewirken sowie Hasslichkeit, Feindschaft, Elend u. a. beheben, entnehmen wir den zitierten colinde das Haar, die Milch, das Blut, und besonders die Knochen."

28. See *Şezătoare* (Fălticeni, 1892), pp. 207-208; see also Alexiu Viciu, *Colinde din Ardeal. Datini de Crăciun şi credinţe poporane. Culegeri cu adnotaţiuni şi glosar* (Bucharest, 1914), p. 65.

29. Monica Bǎrtulescu, *La luncile Soarelui, antologie a colindelor laice* (Bucharest, 1964), p. 113.

30. Elena Niculiţa Voronca, *Dǎţinile şi credinţele poporului român* (Cernǎuţi, 1903), pp. 37-38.

31. *Ţara Nouǎ*, 4 (1887), 612-613.

32. Tudor Pamfile, *Sǎrbǎtorile la Români. Crǎciunul* (Bucharest, 1914), Text 73, p. 85; and, *Folclor din Oltenia şi Muntenia*, 5 (1970), 86-87.

33. I. I. Stoian, "Texte folclorice din Râmnicul Sǎrat," *Grai şi Suflet, Revista Institutului de Filologie şi Folclor*, 3 (1927), 105-107, 122-129.

34. For a more detailed discussion, see Octavian Buhociu, "Folklore and Ethnography in Romania," *Current Anthropology*, 7-8 (1966-67), 295-314.

35. Buhociu, *Mythologie*, p. 22.

36. See Eliade, *Zalmoxis*, pp. 1-4.

37. Jean Przyluski, "Les confrères de loups-garous dans les sociétés Indo-Européennes," *Revue de l'Histoire des Religions*, 121 (1940), 144.

38. Lily Weiser, *Altgermanische Junglingsweihen und Männerbunde* (Baden, 1927); Otto Hofler, *Geheimbunde der Germanen* (Frankfurt, 1934).

39. Stig Wikander, *Der Arische Männerbunde* (Lund, 1938); George Widengren, *Hochgottglaube im alten Iran* (Uppsala, 1938).

CHAPTER IV — DRACULA

1. Emily de Laszowska Gerard, *The Land Beyond the Forest* (Edinburgh & London: Will Blackwood & Sons, 1888), I, 70, 58, 211.

2. Radu Florescu & Raymond T. McNally, *Dracula, A Biography of Vlad the Impaler* (New York: Hawthorn Books, Inc., 1973), p. 174.

3. Bacil F. Kirtley, "Dracula, The Monastic Chronicles and Slavic Folklore," *Midwest Folklore*, 6 (1956), 137.

4. Florescu & McNally, *Dracula*, p. 176.

5. Constantin Eretescu, *Mitologia Românǎ*, a manuscript located at the Institut de Cercetǎri Etnologice şi Dialectologice (Institute of Folklore), Bucharest, Romania, p. 196.

6. Ştefan Andreescu, *Vlad Ţepeş (Dracula) Intre Legendǎ şi Istorie* (Bucharest: Editura Minerva, 1976), p. 276.

7. See Andreescu, *Vlad Țepeș*, p. 277.

8. Raymond McNally & Radu Florescu, *In Search of Dracula* (Greenwich, Connecticut: The New York Graphic Society, 1972).

9. Critobal din Imbros, *Din domnia lui Mahomed al II-lea (anii 1451-1467)*, Vasile Grecu, editor (Bucharest: Editura Academiei, 1963), p. 290, 291; and Laonic Chalcocondil, *Expuneri istorice*, Vasile Grecu, editor (Bucharest: Editura Academiei, 1968), p. 293.

10. Ioan Bogdan, *Scrieri Alese* (Bucharest: Editura Academiei, 1968), p. 468.

11. Andreescu, *Vlad Țepeș*, p. 156.

12. Pavel Chihaia, "Deux armoiries sculptées appartenant aux voivodes Vlad Dracul et Neagod Basarab," *Revue Roumaine d'Histoire de l'Art*, 1, no. 1 (1964), 151-167. Pavel Chihaia, "Steme și simboluri la mânăstirea Argeșului," in *De la Negru Vodă la Neagoe Basarab* (Bucharest: Editura Academiei, 1976).

13. Anton Verancsics, "De situ Transyvanicae Moldaviae et Transalpine," in *Călători straini despre țările române*, (Bucharest: Editura Știinţifică, 1968), I, 399-400.

14. Ioan Bogdan, *Documente privitoare la relaţiile țării românești cu Brașovul și cu țara ungurească în secolul XV și XVI* (Bucharest, 1905), I, no. CCLXV, 323.

CHAPTER V – ROMANIAN FOLK MYTHOLOGY

1. Dumitri Gusti, *Rural Life in Romania* (An Abridged English Version of *La Vie en Roumanie*) (Bucharest, 1914), p. 4.

2. Henri H. Stahl, *Nerej, un village d'une région archaïque*, 3 vols. (Bucharest, 1939); Ion Conea, *Clopotiva, un sat din Hațeg*, 2 vols. (Bucharest, 1940); Traian Herseni, *Unități sociale* (Bucharest, 1944); Ion Ionică, *Reprezentarea cerului* (Bucharest, 1944).

3. Gheorghe Pavelescu, *Cercetări asupra Magiei la Români din Munţii Apuseni* (Bucharest: Institul Social Român, 1945), p. 10.

4. Mihail Cernea, *Monographic Research in Rural Communities in Romanian Sociology* (Vienna: Centre Européen de Sciences Sociales, 1973), p. 35.

5. "Superstition" is a word that my colleague and adviser Cornel Bărbulescu rejects in reference to folk traditions in Romania. My feeling was that despite its suggestion of ignorance and error it is used by folklorists generally with the understanding that the pejorative sense of the word is based on a personal judgment of whether a custom or belief coincides with the speaker's prevailing cultural codes of science, religion, and social interaction; in the same way that what is "myth" to some is "the true word of God" to others. Nevertheless, considering that even within a given body of popular traditions, some beliefs may be less appropriate, one could speak of as "superstition" that which originates in "excessive fear" or "excessive adulation." With this in mind, I agree that in Romania, there are, among the folk traditions, very few superstitions.

6. Pavelescu, *Cercetări*, p. 10.

7. Ştefana Cristescu-Golopenţia, *Gospodăria în credinţele şi riturile magice ale femeilor din Drăguş (Făgăraş)* (Bucharest, 1940), p. 15.

8. Agnes Murgoci, "The Vampire in Romania," *Folk-Lore*, 27, No. 5 (1926), 329.

9. Ovidiu Papadima, *O Viziune Româneasca a lumii* (Bucharest: Collecţia "Convorbiri Literare," 1941), p. 14.

10. A. Nour, *Credinţe, Rituri şi Superstiţii Geto-Dace* (Bucharest: Tipografia Cărţilor Bisericeşti, 1941), p. 6.

11. See Mircea Eliade, *Zalmoxis*, p. 33.

12. See Vasile Pârvan, *Dacia, Civilizaţiile Străvechi din Regiunile Carpato-Danubiene* (Bucharest: Editura Ştiinţifică, 1958), p. 101.

13. Nour, *Credinţe*, p. 66.

14. Eliade, *Zalmoxis*, p. 69.

15. Papadima, *Viziune*, p. 72.

16. Simion Florea Marian, *Sărbătorile*, II, 40ff.

17. Marcel Olinescu, *Mitologie Romînească* (Bucharest: "Casa Scoalelor," 1944), p. 407.

18. Pavelescu, *Cercetări*, p. 41.

19. See also Cristescu-Golopenţia, *Gospodăria*, p. 47.

20. Pavelescu, *Cercetări*, p. 37.

21. Olinescu, *Mitologie*, p. 407, and Papadima, *Viziune*, p. 17.

22. Ion Conea, *Clopotiva un sat din Haţeg*, p. 450.

23. Olinescu, *Mitologie*, p. 407; see also Artur Gorovei, *Credinţi şi Superstiţii ale poporului român* (Bucharest: Librăriile SOCEC, 1915), p. 172.

- 24. Gorovei, *Credinți*, item no. 1966, p. 172.

25. Olinescu, *Mitologie*, p. 407; see also Agnes Murgoci, "Vampire," p. 333.

26. Henri H. Stahl, *Nerej*, p. 311.

27. Mihai Pop, "Modèles de la structure sémantique des textes des cérémonies," *Actes du Premier Congrès International des Linguistes*, Bucharest, 26 août-2 septembre, 2 (1967), 672.

28. See Cristescu-Golopenția, *Gospodaria*, p. 24. See also At. M. Marinescu, "Pricolicii," *Familia*, Anul VIII, (1872), p. 116.

29. See Olinescu, *Mitologie*, p. 445.

30. See Cristescu-Golopenția, *Gospodăria*, p. 24.

31. See Cristescu-Golopenția, p. 59 and Olinescu, p. 445.

32. See Ovidiu Bîrlea, *Mica Enciclopedie a poveștilor Românești* (Bucharest: Editura Științifică și Enciclopedia, 1976), p. 383. Bîrlea has compiled data from B. P. Hașdeu's questionnaire of the late nineteenth century, and Niculița-Voronca's study of 1903.

33. See Marinescu, "Pricoliciii," p. 116.

34. See G. I. Pitiș, "Siște, pricolici, necuratu," *Revista Nouă*, Anul III, Nos. 9 & 10, (1890), p. 392.

35. See Cristescu-Golopenția, p. 59.

36. See Bîrlea, *Enciclopedie*, p. 383, Olinescu, p. 445, Pavelescu, p. 34, and Pitiș, "Siște," p. 392.

37. See Bîrlea, p. 383.

38. See Bîrlea, p. 383.

39. See Cristescu-Golopenția, p. 93.

40. See Olinescu, p. 496.

41. See Bîrlea, p. 383.

42. See Pavelescu, *Cercetări*, in which a cart wheel rolling among the cows signifies a witch is taking their milk, p. 68.

43. In Cristescu-Golopenția, p. 24, the tail may be derived from the *ursitoare*. See also Bîrlea, p. 383, and Olinescu, p. 495.

44. See N. I. Dumitrascu, *Strigoii din credințele, datinile și povestirile poporului Român* (Bucharest: Cultură Natională, 1929), p. 15.

45. The same suggestion was recorded in the studies of Bîrlea, p. 383 (one should eat the garlic); see also Olinescu, p. 407, Pavelescu, p. 66, Dumitrascu, *Strigoii*, p. 15, and Murgoci, p. 334.

46. See Murgoci, p. 308, and Bîrlea, p. 385.

47. See Murgoci, p. 330 for breaking the caul, and Bîrlea, p. 384.

48. See Cristescu-Golopenția, p. 93.

49. See Gorovei, *Credinți*, p. 171 (Saint Peter), Papadima, pp. 22 & 66 (Saint Elijah and Saint Nicholas), Olinescu, p. 371 (Saint Peter).

50. See Stahl, *Nerej*, p. 95.
51. See Olinescu, p. 378.
52. See Gorovei, p. 172.
53. Dumitrascu, p. 15.
54. Bîrlea, p. 383.
55. Pavelescu, p. 66.

CHAPTER VI: ROMANIAN PARALLELS

1. Wilhelm Hertz, *Der Werwolf* (Stuttgart, 1862), p. 236; cited in W. R. S. Ralston, *Russian Folk-Tales* (London: Smith & Elder & Co., 1873), p. 318.

2. Ian Woodward, *The Vampire Delusion* (N.Y.: Paddington Press, Ltd., 1979), pp. 50-53.

3. Ralston, *Folk-Tales*, p. 385. See also, Kirby F. Smith, "An Historical Study of the Werwolf in Literature," *PMLA*, 9 (1894), 32.

4. S. Karl, *Danziger Sagen* (Danzig, 1844), II, 38.

5. Jacob Grim, *Teutonic Mythology*, trans. James Steven Stallybrass (London: George Bell & Sons, 1883), III, 1094.

6. John Cuthbert Lawson, *Modern Greek Folklore and Ancient Greek Religion* (New Hyde Park, New York: University Books, 1964), p. 384.

7. Roman Jakobson, *Slavic Epic Studies*, Selected Writings 4, (Paris: Nouton & Co., 1966), p. 345.

8. *The Russian Primary Chronicle*, trans. Samuel H. Cross, *Harvard Studies and Notes in Philology and Literature* (Cambridge, 1930), XII, p. 288.

9. Jakobson, *Studies*, p. 342.

10. James G. Frazer, *The Golden Bough* (New York: The Macmillan Co., 1918, I, 187, 199ff.

11. Jakobson, *Studies*, p. 349.

12. Josef Cizmar, *Lidove Lekarstvi v Ceskoslovensku* (Brno: Melantrich A. S., 1946), I, 287.

13. Jan Machal, *Slavic Mythology of All Races* (New York: Cooper Square Publishers Inc., 1964), III, 229.

14. F. S. Copeland, "Slovene Folklore," *Folk-Lore*, 42 (1931), 425.

15. Machal, *Slavic Mythology*, p. 229; Edmund Schneeweiss, *Serbo-kroatische Volkskunde* (Berlin: Walter de Gruyter Co., 1961), I, 10.

16. Copeland, "Slovene Folklore," p. 414.

17. Schneeweis, *Volkskunde*, p. 14.

18. Machal, *Slavic Mythology*, p. 287.

19. Cizmar, *Lekarstvi*, I, p. 287.

20. Samuel X. Radbill, M.D., "The Folklore of Teething," *Keystone Folklore Quarterly*, 9, (1964), p. 125.

21. W.R.S. Ralston, *The Songs of the Russian People* (London: Ellis & Green, 1872), pp. 409, 412. See also, Machal, *Slavic Mythology*, p. 230; Schneeweis, *Volkskunde*, I, 8; Khristo Vakarelski, *Bulgarische Volkskunde* (Berlin: Walter De Gruyter, 1969), p. 239.

22. Ralston, *Songs*, pp. 409-410.

23. Ralston, *Russian Folk-Tales*, p. 321-322. See also, Vakarelski, *Bulgarische Volkskunde*, p. 239; Machal, *Slavic Mythology*, p. 232; Radbill, "Teething," p. 125; Schneeweis, *Volkskunde*, I, 9.

24. Ralston, *Folk-Tales*, p. 232.

25. Machal, *Slavic Mythology*, p. 232; Vakarelski, *Bulgarische Volkskunde*, p. 305; Cizmar, *Lekarstvi*, I, 287; Schneeweis, *Volkskunde*, I, 9.

26. Sula Benet, *Song, Dance and Customs of Peasant Poland* (London: Dennis Hobson, n.d.), p. 238.

27. Schneeweis, *Volkskunde*, I, 9.

28. Schneeweis, *Volkskunde*, I, 9; Copeland, "Slovene Folklore," p. 428; Machal, *Slavic Mythology*, p. 230; Vakarelski, *Bulgarische Volkskunde*, p. 240.

29. Radbill, "Teething," p. 125; Schneeweis, *Volkskunde*, I, 9.

30. Cizmar, *Lekarstvi*, I, 9.

31. Ralston, *Songs*, p. 412; Schneeweis, *Volkskunde*, I, 9.

32. Copeland, "Slovene Folklore," p. 429..

33. Ralston, *Folk-Tales*, p. 290.

34. Lawson, *Modern Greek Folklore*, p. 375.

35. Richard & Eva Blum, *The Dangerous Hour: The Lore of Crisis and Mystery in Rural Greece* (New York: Charles Scribners, 1970), p. 70.

36. D. Demetracopoulou Lee, "Greek Accounts of the Vrykolakas," *Journal of American Folklore*, 55 (1942), 128.

37. Lynwood Carranco, "A Miscellany of Folk Beliefs from the Redwood Country," *Western Folklore*, 26 (1967), 172.

38. Grace Partridge Smith, "Folklore from Egypt," *JAF*, 54 (1941), 51.

39. Arthur Palmer Hudson & Pete Kyle McCarter, "The Bell Witch of Tennessee and Mississippi: A Folk Legend," *JAF*, 47 (1934), p.

62-63; Joseph D. Clark, "Superstitions from North Carolina," *Southern Folklore Quarterly*, 26 (1962), 220.

40. Mody C. Boatright, Wilson M. Hudson, & Allen Maxwell, eds., *The Golden Log* (Dallas, Texas Southern Methodist University Press, 1962), Publications of the Texas Folklore Society, No. 31, p. 115.

41. Machal, *Slavic Mythology*, p. 230.

42. Marthe Moricet, "Traditions populaires de la Normandie, Le Varou," *Annales de Normandie*, 2 (1952), 75.

43. Erika Bourguignon, "The Persistence of Folk Belief: Some Notes on Cannibalism and Zombies in Haiti," *JAF*, 72 (1959), 39.

44. Zora Hurston, "Hoodoo in America," *JAF*, 44 (1931), 321.

45. Will-Erich Peuckert, *Deutsche Sagen I. Niederdeutschland* (Berlin: Erich Schmidt Verlag, 1961), p. 114.

46. M. Edith Durham, "Of Magic, Witches and Vampires in the Balkans," *Man*, 23 (1923), 190 & 192.

47. Dudley Wright, *Vampires and Vampirism* (London: Will, Rider & Son, 1924), p. 157.

48. Maximo Ramos, "The Aswang Syncrasy in Philippine Folklore," *Western Folklore*, 28 (1969), pp. 238-243.

49. Amélie Bosquet, *La Normandie romanesque et merveilleuse* (Paris, 1845), p. 238.

50. Paul Sébillot, *Folklore de France* (Paris: Maisonneuve et Larose, 1968), IV, 210.

51. Hertz, *Werwolf*, p. 70.

52. Montague Summers, *The Werewolf* (London: Kegan Paul, Trench, Trubner & Co., Ltd., 1933), p. 185.

53. Bosquet, *La Normandie*, p. 232; Moricet, "Traditions,", p. 81.

54. Summers, *Werewolf*, p. 222; Sébillot, *Folklore*, III, 55; also A. Durand-Tullou, *Du Chien au Loup-Garou dans le fantastique de Claude Seignolle* (Paris: G. P. Maisonneuve, 1961), p. 164.

55. Sébillot, *Folklore*, III, 55.

56. Durand-Tullou, *Du Chien*, p. 160.

57. Sébillot, *Folklore*, I, 285.

58. Durand-Tullou, *Du Chien*, p. 163.

59. Summers, *Werewolf*, p. 164.

60. Sébillot, *Folklore*, III, 55.

61. Summers, *Werewolf*, p. 222; Durand-Tullou, *Du Chien*, p. 160.

62. Moricet, "Traditions," p. 81.

63. Sébillot, *Folklore*, I, 285 and III, 143, 55; Durand-Tullou, *Du Chien*, p. 164.

64. Louis C. Jones, "Italian Werewolves," *New York Folklore Quarterly*, 6 (1950), 134, 136.

65. Hertz, *Werwolf*, p. 82.

66. Vincente Risco, "El 'Lobishome'," *Revista de Dialectologia y Tradiciones Populares*, I (1945), 526; José Diego Ribeiro, "Turquel Folklorico," *Revista Lusitana*, 20 (1917), 60.

67. Durand-Tullou, *Du Chien*, p. 165.

68. Sébillot, *Folklore*, I, 284.

69. Durand-Tullou, *Du Chien*, p; 87-88.

70. Summers, *Werewolf*, p. 163; Jones, "Italian Werewolves,", p. 137.

71. Smith, "Werewolf in literature," p. 35.

72. Summers, *Werewolf*, p. 163; Jones, "Italian Werewolves," p. 135.

73. Eisler, *Man Into Wolf*, p. 152; Taylor, *Primitive Culture*, I, 281.

74. Eisler, *Man Into Wolf*, p. 155.

75. *Encyclopedia of Religion & Ethics*, James Hastings, ed. (New York: Charles Scribners & Sons, 1922), VIII, 207.

76. Antoine Cabaton, "Le Loup-Garou en Indochine et en Indonesie," *L'Ethnographie*, new series, No. 6, 1922, p. 56-58.

77. Summers, *Werewolf*, p. 166.

78. *Encyclopedia of Religion & Ethics*, VIII, 209; Ribeiro, "Turquel Folklorico," p. 60; Risco, "El 'Lobishome'," p. 526.

79. Jan C. Perkowski, *Vampires of the Slavs* (Cambridge, Massachusetts: Slavica Publishers, Inc., 1976), p. 137.

BIBLIOGRAPHY

1. Alford, Violet. *Pyrenean Festivals*. London: Chatto & Windus, 1937.

2. ———— —— and Rodney Gallop. *The Traditional Dance*. London: Methuen & Co., 1935.

3. Amzulescu, I. *Balade populare românești*. 2 volumes. Bucharest, 1964.

4. ———— ————. "Cântecul nostru bătrânesc," *Revista de Folclor*, 5 (1960), 25-58.

5. Andreescu, Ștefan. *Vlad Țepeș (Dracula) Intre Legendă și Istorie*. Bucharest: Editura Minerva, 1976.

6. Baring-Gould, Sabine. *The Book of Were-wolves*. London: Smith Elder & Co., 1865.

7. Bîrlea, Ovidiu. *Mica Enciclopedie a poveștilor românești*. Bucharest: Editura Științifică și Enciclopedica, 1976.

8. Blum, Richard and Eva. *The Dangerous Hour: The Lore of Crisis and Mystery in Rural Greece*. New York: Charles Scribner's Sons, 1970.

9. Bodin, Jean. *De la démonomanie des sorciers*. Paris, 1587.

10. Bosquet, Amélie. *La Normandie romanesque et merveilleuse*. Paris, 1845.

11. Bourguignon, Erika. "The Persistence of Folk Belief: Some Notes on Cannibalism and Zombies in Haiti," *Journal of American Folklore*, 72 (1959), 36-46.

12. Brown, Peter, "Sorcery, Demons and the Rise of Christianity from Late Antiquity into the Middle Ages," in Mary Douglas, editor, *Witchcraft Confessions and Accusations*. London: Tavistock Publications, 1970, pp. 17-45.

13. Buhociu, Octovian. *Die Rumänische Volkskultur und ihre Mythologie*. Wiesbaden: Otto Harrassowitz, 1974.

14. ———————. "Folklore and Ethnography in Romania," *Current Anthropology*, 7-8 (1966-67), 295-314.

15. Cabaton, Antoine. "Le Loup-Garou en Indochine et en Indonesie," *L'Ethnographie*, New Series No. 6 (1922), pp. 55-58.

16. Carranco, Lynwood. "A Miscellany of Folk Beliefs from the Redwood Country," *Western Folklore*, 26 (1967), 169-176.

17. Cernea, Mihail. *Monographic Research in Rural Communities in Romanian Sociology.* Vienna: Centre Européen de Sciences Sociales, 1973.

18. Clark, Joseph D. "Superstitions from North Carolina, *Southern Folklore Quarterly,* 26 (1967), 198-224.

19. Cizmar, Joseph. *Lidove Lekarstvi v Ceskoslovensku.* Brno: Melantrich A. S., 1946. Vol. I.

20. Cohn, Norman. "The Myth of Satan and His Human Servants," in Mary Douglas, editor, *Witchcraft Confessions and Accusations,* pp. 3-16.

21. Cristescu-Golopenția, Ștefana. *Gospodăria în credințele și riturile magice ale femeilor din Drăguș (Făgăraș).* Bucharest, 1940.

22. Douglas, Mary. *Witchcraft Confessions and Accusations.* London: Tavistock Publications, 1970.

23. Dumézil, Georges. *Le Problème des centaures.* Paris: Librairie Orientaliste Paul Geuthner, 1929.

24. —————. *Mythes et dieux des Germains.* Paris, 1939.

25. —————. *The Destiny of the Warrior.* Chicago: University of Chicago Press, 1970.

26. Dumitrașcu, N. I. *Strigoii din credințele, datinile și povestirile poporului român.* Bucharest: Cultura Națională, 1929.

27. Durand-Tullou, A. *Du Chien au loup-garou dans le fantastique de Claude Seignolle.* Paris: G. P. Maisonneuve, 1961.

28. Durham, M. Edith. "Of Magic, Witches and Vampires in the Balkans," *Man,* 23 (1923), 189-192.

29. Eisler, Robert. *Man Into Wolf.* London: Routledge & Kegan Paul Ltd., 1951.

30. Eliade, Mircea. *Occultism, Witchcraft and Cultural Fashions.* Chicago: University of Chicago Press, 1976.

31. —————. *Zalmoxis The Vanishing God.* Chicago: University of Chicago Press, 1972.

32. Eretescu, Constantin. *Mitologia Română.* A manuscript located at the Institutul de Cercetări Etnologice și Dialectologice (Institute of Folklore), Bucharest, Romania.

33. Fiske, John. *Myths and Myth Makers.* New York: Houghton Mifflin Co., 1914.

34. Florescu, Radu and Raymond T. McNally. *Dracula, A Biography of Vlad the Impaler.* New York: Hawthorn Books, Inc., 1973.

35. Fochi, Adrian. *Miriorița: Tipologie, circulație, geneză, texte cu un studi introductiv de Pavel Apostol.* Bucharest, 1964.

36. Fraser, Sir James G. *Ovid's Fasti*. London: Loeb Classical Library, 1951.

37. ――――――. *The Golden Bough*, abridged edition by Theodor H. Gaster. New York: Mentor Books, 1964.

38. Freud, Sigmund. *The Uncanny*. Complete Works. London: The Hogarth Press, 1955. Vol. XVII.

39. Gaignebet, Claude and Marie-Claude Florentin. *Le Carnaval*. Paris: Payot, 1974.

40. Gerard, Emily. *The Land Beyond the Forest*. 2 vols. London: Will Blackwood & Sons, 1888.

41. Gerstein, Mary. "Germanic Warg: The Outlaw as Werewolf," in *Myth in Indo-European Antiquity*, Gerald James Lawson, ed. Berkeley and Los Angeles: University of California Press, 1974, pp. 131-156.

42. "Getae," and "Thrace." *Encyclopedia Brittanica*. 1966 edition.

43. Gorovei, Artur. *Credinţi şi superstiţii ale poporului român*. Bucharest: Librarile SOCEC, 1915.

44. Grimm, Jacob. *Teutonic Mythology*. Trans. James Steven Stallybrass. 4 vols. London: George Bell & Sons, York Street, 1888.

45. Gusti, Dumitri. *Rural Life in Romania*, an abridged English version of *La Vie rurale en Roumanie*. Bucharest, 1914.

46. Hertz, Wilhelm. *Der Werwolf*. Stuttgart, 1862.

47. Hudson, Arthur Palmer and Pete Kyle McCarter. "The Bell Witch of Tennessee and Mississippi: A Folk Legend," *Journal of American Folklore*, 47 (1934),45-63.

48. Hurston, Zora. "Hoodoo in America," *Journal of American Folklore*, 44 (1931), 317-417.

49. Ionică, Ion. *Reprezentarea cerului*. Bucharest, 1944.

50. Iroai, Petru. "Miorita o il canto della fusione con la Natura," *Folklore*, 12 (Naples, 1958), 34-42.

51. Jakobson, Roman. *Slavic Epic Studies*. Selected Writings IV. Paris: Mouton & Co., 1966.

52. Jakobson, Svatava Pirkova. "Slavic Folklore," *Standard Dictionary of Folklore and Mythology*. 1972 edition.

53. Jones, Ernest. *Nightmare, Witches and Devils*. New York, 1931.

54. Jones, Louis C. "Italian Werewolves," *New York Folklore Quarterly*, 6 (1950), 133-138.

55. Karl, S. *Danziger Sagen*. 2 vols. Danzig, 1844.

56. Kirby, E. T. "The Origin of the Mummers' Play," *Journal of American Folklore*, 84 (1971), 275-288.

57. Kirtley, Bacil F. "Dracula, The Monastic Chronicles and Slavic Folklore," *Midwest Folklore*, 6 (1956), 133-139.

58. Lawson, John Cuthbert. *Modern Greek Folklore and Ancient Greek Religion*. New Hyde Park, New York: University Books, 1964.

59. Leandicho-Lopez, Mellie. "Philippine and Slavic Vampires," a paper read at the International Symposium on Creatures of Legendry, The University of Nebraska at Omaha, September 28 to October 1, 1978.

60. Lee, D. Demetracopoulou. "Greek Accounts of the Vryko-lakas," *Journal of American Folklore*, 55 (1942), 126-132.

61. Lienhardt, R. G. "Some Notions of Witchcraft among the Dinka," *Africa*, 21 (1951), 4: 303-318.

62. MacCulloch, J. A. "Lycanthropy," and "Vampire." *Encyclopedia of Religion and Ethics*. 1922 edition.

63. Machal, Jan. *Slavic Mythology*. Mythology of All Races, Vol. III. New York: Cooper Square Publishers, Inc., 1964.

64. Marinescu, At. M. "Pricolicii," *Familia*, anul VIII (1872).

65. Marx, Jean. *L'Inquisition en Dauphiné*. Paris: Honoré Champion, 1914.

66. McNally, Raymond T. and Radu Florescu. *In Search of Dracula*. Greenwich, Connecticut: New York Graphic Society, 1972.

67. Megas, George. *Greek Calendar Customs*. Athens: Prime Minister's Office, 1958.

68. Moldoveanu-Nestor, Elisabeta. "Sărbătoarea secerešului," *Revista de Etnografie și Folclor*, 1964, pp. 615-634.

69. Morgan, William. *Human Wolves among the Navaho*. Yale University Publications in Anthropology, no. 11. New Haven: Yale University Press, 1936.

70. Murgoci, Agnes. "The Vampire in Romania," *Folk-Lore*, 27, no. 5 (1926), 320-349.

71. Niculița-Voronca, Elena. *Datinele și credințele poporului român*. Cernăuți, 1903.

72. Nour, A. *Credințe, rituri și superstiții Geto-Dace*. Bucharest: Tipografia Cărților Bisericești, 1941.

73. Olinescu, Marcel. *Mitologie Romînească*. Bucharest: "Casa Școalelor," 1944.

74. Oprișan, Horia Barbu. *Monografia folclorica a Teleormanului*. Bucharest: Casa Creației Populare a Teleormanului, 1971.

75. Pamfile, Tudor. *Sărbătorile la Români. Crăciunul*. Bucharest, 1914.

76. Papadima, Ovidiu. *O viziune româneasca a lumii*. Bucharest: Colecția "Convorbiri Literare," 1941.

77. Pârvan, Vasile. *Dacia, Civilizații Strǎvechi din Regiunile Carpato-Danubiene*. Bucharest: Editura Științificǎ, 1958.

78. ———————. *Getica, o protohistorie a Daciei*. Bucharest, 1926.

79. Pavelescu, Gheorghe. *Cercetǎri asupra Magiei la Românii din Munții Apuseni*. Bucharest: Institutul Social Român, 1945.

80. Perkowski, Jan. *Vampires of the Slavs*. Cambridge, Massachusetts: Slavica Publishers, Inc., 1976.

81. Peuckert, Will-Erich. *Deutsche Sagen*. Berlin: Erich Schmidt Verlag, 1961. Vol. I, Niederdeutschland.

82. Pitiș, G. I. "Siște, Pricolici, Necurații," *Revista Nouǎ*, anul III, nos. 9 & 10 (1890), pp. 391-393.

83. Pluquet, Frederic. *Contes populaires, préjugés, patois et proverbes*. Caen, 1834.

84. Pop, Mihai. "Modèles de la structure sémantique des textes de cérémonies," *Actes du Premier Congrès International des Linguistes*, Bucharest, August 26- September 2, 1967, pp. 667-678.

85. Przyluski, Jean. "Les Confréries de loup-garous dans les sociétés indo-européennes," *Revue de l'Histoire des Religions*, 121 (1940), 128-145.

86. Radbill, Samuel X., M. D. "The Folklore of Teething," *Keystone Folklore Quarterly*, 9 (1964), 123-143,

87. Ralston, W.R.S. *Russian Folk-Tales*. London: Smith Elder & Co., 1873.

88. ———————. *The Songs of the Russian People*. London: Ellis & Green, 1872.

89. Ramos, Maximo. "The Aswang Syncrasy in Philippine Folklore," *Western Folklore*, 28 (1969), 238-248.

90. Risco, Vincente. "El 'Lobishome'," *Revista de Dialectologia y Tradiciones Populares*, I (1945), 514-533.

91. Ruel, Malcolm. "Were-animals and the Introverted Witch among the Dinka," in, Mary Douglas, editor, *Witchcraft Confessions and Accusations*, pp. 333-350.

92. Schmidt, Bernhard. *Das Volkslegender Neugriechen*. Leipzig, 1871. Vol. I.

93. Schneeweis, Edmund. *Serbokroatische Volkskunde*. Berlin: Walter de Gruyter Co., 1961. Vol. I.

94. Sébillot, Paul. *Folklore de France*. 4 vols. Paris: Maisonneuve et Larose, 1968.

95. Seyffert, Oscar. *Dictionary of Classical Antiquities*, revised and edited by Henry Nettleship and J. E. Sandys. New York: Meridian Books, 1962.

96. Senn, Harry. "Some Were-Wolf Legends and the *Căluşari* Ritual in Romania," *East European Quarterly*, 11, no. 1 (1977), 1-14.

97. Smith, Grace Partridge. "Folklore from 'Egypt'." *Journal of American Folklore*, 54 (1941), 48-59.

98. Smith, Kirby F. "An Historical Study of the Werwolf in Literature," *PMLA*, 9 (1894), 1-42.

99. Stahl, Henri H. *Nerej, un village d'une région archaïque*. 3 vols. Bucharest, 1939.

100. Stoian, I. I. "Texte folclorice din Râmnicul Sărat," *Grai şi Suflet, Revista Institutului de Filogie şi Folklor*, 3 (1927), 105-107.

101. Summers, Montague. *The Werewolf*. London: Kegan Paul, 1933.

102. Tylor, Edward B. *Primitive Culture*. London: John Murray, 1885. Vol. I.

103. Vakarelski, Khristo. *Bulgarische Volkskunde*. Berlin: Walter de Gruyter Co., 1969.

104. Woodward, Ian. *The Vampire Delusion*. New York: Paddington Press Ltd., 1979.

105. Wright, Dudley. *Vampires and Vampirism*. London: Will Rider & Son, 1924.

INDEX

EAST EUROPEAN MONOGRAPHS

The *East European Monographs* comprise scholarly books on the history and civilization of Eastern Europe. They are published by the *East European Quarterly* in the belief that these studies contribute substantially to the knowledge of the area and serve to stimulate scholarship and research.

Political Ideas and the Enlightenment in the Romanian Principalities, 17501831. By Vlad Georgescu. 1971.
America, Italy and the Birth of Yugoslavia, 1917-1919. By Dragan R. Zivjinovic. 1972.
Jewish Nobles and Geniuses in Modern Hungary. By William O. McCagg,Jr. 1972.
Mixail Soloxov in Yugoslavia: Reception and Literary Impact. By Robert F. Price. 1973.
The Historical and National Thought of Nicolae Iorga. By William O. Oldson. 1973.
Guide to Polish Libraries and Archives. By Richard C. Lewanski. 1974.
Vienna Broadcasts to Slovakia, 1938-1939: A Case Study in Subversion. By Henry Delfiner. 1974.
The 1917 Revolution in Latvia. By Andrew Ezergailis. 1974.
The Ukraine in the United Nations Organization: A Study in Soviet Foreign Policy. 1944-1950. By Konstantin Sawczuk. 1975.
The Bosnian Church: A New Interpretation. By John V. A. Fine, Jr., 1975.
Intellectual and Social Developments in the Habsburg Empire from Maria Theresa to World War I. Edited by Stanley B. Winters and Joseph Held. 1975.
Ljudevit Gaj and the Illyrian Movement. By Elinor Murray Despalatovic. 1975.
Tolerance and Movements of Religious Dissent in Eastern Europe. Edited by Bela K. Kiraly. 1975.
The Polish Republic: Hlinka's Slovak People's Party, 19391945. By Yeshayahu Jelinek. 1976.
The Russian Annexation of Bessarabia, 1774-1828. By George F. Jewsbury. 1976.
Modern Hungarian Historiography. By Steven Bela Vardy. 1976.
Values and Community in Multi-National Yugoslavia. By Gary K. Bertsch. 1976.
The Greek Socialist Movement and the First World War: the Road to unity. By George B. Leon. 1976.
The Radical Left in the Hungarian Revolution of 1848. By Laszlo Deme. 1976.
Hungary between Wilson and Lenin: The Hungarian Revolution of 1918-1919 and the Big Three. By Peter Pastor. 1976.
The Crises of France's East-Central European Diplomacy, 1933-1938. By Anthony J. Komjathy. 1976.
Polish Politics and National aReform, 1775-1788. By Daniel Stone. 1976.
The Habsburg Empire in World War I. Robert A. Kann, Bela K. Kiraly, and Paula S. Fichtner, eds. 1977.
The Slovenes and Yugoslavism, 1890-1914. By Carole Rogel. 1977.
German-Hungarian Relations and the Swabian Problem. By Thomas Spira. 1977.
The Metamorphosis of a Social Class in Hungary During the Reign of Young Franz Joseph. By Peter I. Hidas. 1977.
Tax Reform in Eighteenth Century Lombardy. By Daniel M. Klang. 1977.
Tradition versus Revolution: Russia and the Balkans in 1917. By Robert H. Johnston. 1977.
Winter into Spring: The Czechoslovak Press and the Reform Movement 19631968. By Frank L. Kaplan. 1977.
The Catholic Church and the Soviet Government, 1939-1949. By Dennis J. Dunn. 1977.
The Hungarian Labor Service System, 1939-1945. By Randolph L. Braham. 1977.
Consciousness and History: Nationalist Critics of Greek Society 1897-1914. By Gerasimos Augustinos. 1977.
Emigration in Polish Social and Political Thought, 1870-1914. By Benjamin P. Murdzek. 1977.
Serbian Poetry and Milutin Bojic. By Mihailo Dordevic. 1977.
The Baranya Dispute: Diplomacy in the Vortex of Ideologies, 1918-1921. By Leslie C. Tihany. 1978.
The United States in Prague, 1945-1948. By Walter Ullmann. 1978.
Rush to the Alps: The Evolution of Vacationing in Switzerland. By Paul P. Bernard. 1978.
Transportation in Eastern Europe: Empirical Findings. By Bogdan Mieczkowski. 1978.
The Polish Underground State: A Guide to the Underground, 1939-1945. By Stefan Korbonski. 1978.
The Hungarian Revolution of 1956 in Retrospect. Edited by Bela K. Kiraly and Paul Jonas. 1978.
Boleslaw Limanowski (1835-1935): A Study in Socialism and Nationalism. By Kazimiera Janina Cottam. 1978.
The Lingering Shadow of Nazism: The Austrian Independent Party Movement Since 1945. By Max E. Riedlsperger. 1978.
The Catholic Church, Dissent and Nationality in Soviet Lithuania. By V. Stanley Vardys. 1978.
The Development of Parliamentary Government in Serbia. By Alex N. Dragnich. 1978.
Divide and Conquer: German Efforts to Conclude a Separate Peace, 1914-1918. By L. L. Farrar, Jr. 1978.
The Prague Slav Congress of 1848. By Lawrence D. Orton. 1978.
The Nobility and the Making of the Hussite Revolution. By John M. Klassen. 1978.
The Cultural Limits of Revolutionary politics: Change and Continuity in Socialist Czechoslovakia. By David W. Paul. 1979.
On the Border of War and Peace: Polish Intelligence and Diplomacy in 19371939 and the Origins of the Ultra Secret. By Richard A. Woytak. 1979.
Bear and Foxes: The International Relations of the East European States 19651969. By Ronald Haly Linden. 1979.

Czechoslovakia: The Heritage of Ages Past. Edited by Ivan Volgyes and Hans Brisch. 1979.

Prima Minister Gyula Andrassy's Influence on Habsburg Foreign Policy. By Janos Decsy. 1979.

Citizens for the Fatherland: Education, Educators, and Pedagogical Ideals in Eighteenth Century Russia. By J. L. Black. 1979.

A History of the "Proletariat": The Emergence of Marxism in the Kingdom of Poland, 1870-1887. By Norman M. Naimark. 1979.

The Slovak Autonomy Movement, 1935-1939: A Study in Unrelenting Nationalism. By Dorothea H. El Mallakh. 1979.

Diplomat in Exile: Francis Pulszky's Political Activities in England, 1849-1860. By Thomas Kabdebo. 1979.

The German Struggle Against the Yugoslav Guerrillas in World War II: German Counter-Insurgency in Yugoslavia, 1941-1943. By Paul N. Hehn. 1979.

The Emergence of the Romanian National State. By Gerald J. Bobango. 1979.

Stewards of the Land: The American Farm School and Modern Greece. By Brenda L. Marder. 1979.

Roman Dmowski: Party, Tactics, Ideology, 1895-1907. By Alvin M. Fountain, II. 1980.

International and Domestic Politics in Greece During the Crimean War. By Jon V. Kofas. 1980.

Fires on the Mountain: The Macedonian Revolutionary Movement and the Kidnapping of Ellen Stone. By Laura Beth Sherman. 1980.

The Modernization of Agriculture: Rural Transformation in Hungary, 1848-1975. Edited by Joseph Held. 1980.

Britain and the War for Yugoslavia, 1940-1943. By Mark C. Wheeler. 1980.

The Turn to the Right: The Ideological Origins and Development of Ukrainian Nationalism, 1919-1929. By Alexander J. Motyl. 1980.

The Maple Leaf and the White Eagle: Canadian-Polish Relations, 1918-1978. By Aloysius Balawyder. 1980.

Antecedents of Revolution: Alexander I and the Polish Congress Kingdom, 1815-1825. By Frank W. Thackeray. 1980.

Blood Libel at Tiszaeszlar. By Andrew Handler. 1980.

Democratic Centralism in Romania: A Study of Local Communist Politics. By Daniel N. Nelson. 1980.

The Challenge of Communist Education: A Look at the German Democratic Republic. By Margrete Siebert Klein. 1980.

The Fortifications and Defense of Constantinople. By Byron C.P. Tsangadas. 1980.

Balkan Cultural Studies. By Stavro Skendi. 1980.

Studies in Ethnicity: The East European Experience in America. Edited by Charles A. Ward, Philip Shahshko, and Donald E. Pienkos. 1980.

The Logic of "Normalization:" The Soviet Intervention in Czechoslovakia and the Czechoslovak Response. By Fred Eidlin. 1980.

Red Cross. Black Eagle: A Biography of Albania's American Schol. By Joan Fultz Kontos. 1981.

Nationalism in Contemporary Europe. By Franjo Tudjman. 1981.

Great Power Rivalry at the Turkish Straits: The Montreux Conference and Convention of 1936. By Anthony R. DeLuca. 1981.

Islam Under the Double Eagle: The Muslims of Bosnia and Hercegovina, 1878-1914. By Robert J. Donia. 1981.

Five Eleventh Century Hungarian Kings: Their Policies and Their Relations with Rome. By Z.J. Kosztolnyik. 1981.

Prelude to Appeasement: East European Central Diplomacy in the Early 1930's. By Lisanne Radice. 1981.

The Soviet Regime in Czechoslovakia. By Zdenek Krystufek. 1981.

School Strikes in Prussian Poland, 1901-1907: The Struggle Over Bilingual Education. By John J. Kulczycki. 1981.

Romantic Nationalism and Liberalism: Joachim Lelewel and the Polish National Idea. By Joan S. Skurnowicz. 1981.

The "Thaw" In Bulgarian Literature. By Atanas Slavov. 1981.

The Political Thought of Thomas G. Masaryk. By roman Szporluk. 1981.

Prussian Poland in the German Empire, 1871-1900. By Richard Blanke. 1981.

The Mazepists: Ukrainian Separatism in the Early Eighteenth Century. By Orest Subtelny. 1981.

The Battle for the Marchlands: The Russo-Polish Campaign of 1920. By Adam Zamoyski. 1981.

Milovan Djilas: A Revolutionary as a Writer. By Dennis Reinhartz. 1981.

DATE DUE

MAY 1 7 2004			
MAY 0 7 2004		JUL 1 4 2010	
OCT 1 7 2005			
OCT 2 7 2005			
FEB 1 5 2010			
GAYLORD			PRINTED IN U.S.A.